BLACK IN TWO WORLDS:
A PERSONAL PERSPECTIVE ON HIGHER EDUCATION

CARL A. FIELDS

red|HummingbirdPress

Princeton, New Jersey

Two articles were adapted from the book and appeared in the April 18,1977 and April 25,
1977 issues of the *Princeton Alumni Weekly*; they also appeared in *The Best of PAW:
100 years of the Princeton Alumni Weekly*, edited by J.I. Merritt.

Published by Red Hummingbird Press, L.L.C.
PO Box 462, Princeton, New Jersey 08542

www.redhummingbirdpress.com

Publisher's Cataloging-in-Publication
(Provided by Quality Books, Inc.)

Fields, Carl A.
    Black in two worlds : a personal perspective on
higher education / by Carl A. Fields.
    p. cm.
    ISBN 0-9727310-6-7

    1. Fields, Carl A. 2. Princeton University--Administration--
Biography. 3. University of Zambia--Administration--Biography.
4. African American college administrators--Biography.
5. Discrimination in higher education--United States--History--20th
century. 6. African Americans--Civil rights. 7. African Americans--
Politics and government. 8. Blacks--Zambia--Civil rights. 9. Blacks--
Zambia--Politics and government. 10. Civil rights movements--United
States--History--20th century. 11. Self-determination, National--
Zambia--History--20th century. 12. Zambia--Social conditions--
1964- 13. United States--Social conditions--1960-1980. 14. Zambia--
Race relations. 15. United States--Race relations. I. Title.

LD4606.F54A3 2006   378'.0092
                                           QBI05-600208

ISBN-13: 978-0-972-7310-6-7
ISBN-10: 0-972-7310-6-7

Book Layout by Lara Edwards
Printed in the United States of America

BLACK IN TWO WORLDS

Charles W. Daves, Editor

Foreword by Robert F. Goheen

Afterword by Badi G. Foster

BLACK IN TWO WORLDS

FOREWORD

When Carl Fields was persuaded to join the administration of
Princeton University during the summer of 1964, it needed his rare
combination of penetrating insight, carefully considered persuasive-
ness, and firm although low-key tenacity more than it knew at the
time–and probably more even than Carl in his most candid mood may
have envisioned. It is this phase of his life, his seven years at Princeton,
that form the first half (almost exactly) of this, his memoir, *Black in
Two Worlds*, and it is the phase of his life in which I could observe his
work at close range and would come to know him as a colleague and
friend.

Of his experiences and accomplishments in that other very
different "world" of the fledging University of Zambia, I know only
what he tells us here plus a few reminiscences he shared following his
return to the United States. But clearly Carl as University Planning
Officer made a unique and telling contribution there, too, through
much the same combination of qualities: his ability to see into and
understand how others feel and are motivated, a sensitive yet firm
grasp of what was at stake, calm determination to achieve a construc-
tive result–all, underlying and buttressing considerable administrative
skill.

Not only had the 200-plus-year-old Princeton that Carl joined in
1964 been notoriously slow in granting admission to black students,
most of us who ran it had until very recently remained largely
oblivious to the widespread, grinding humiliation imposed on blacks,
especially in the South but not only there, under the banner and
blanket of white supremacy. That was so until, highlighted by TV and
also brought close by the participation of some of our own students,
the civil rights uprisings of the late 1950s and early 1960s woke us up.
Certainly for me these developments proved to be both an eye-opener
and call to action.

The first black student since the 18th century to break Princeton's color barrier was a carry-over from one of the military officer training programs conducted by the University during World War II, and it may have helped that he was a fine basketball player. By 1961 when we had become sufficiently aroused to be actively seeking black applicants, only two more had enrolled. To our surprise we discovered that various things in its history made Princeton a less-than-attractive prospect for many young blacks well qualified for enrollment, while for those who took the chance and enrolled it was proving to be a less-than-comfortable setting.

Such was the situation that led us to decide to reach out for help that might be gained by bringing an experienced black man into our effort. How fortunate Princeton was that the broad outside contacts and keen judgment of Bradford Craig, Director of Financial Aid, identified Carl Fields at Teachers College, Columbia as possibly available and successfully persuaded him to join his staff! From almost the moment of his arrival, Carl, while carrying on all the normal duties of a financial aid officer, became active both in helping to identify and attract black applicants and in helping those who enrolled to maintain their self-esteem and cope more readily with the often unfamiliar, academically intense, socially very white environment in which they found themselves immersed.

When Carl left Princeton, it was by no means a place of perfect inter-racial harmony. Nor is it such even today. But it had come a long way toward being an institution in which young men and women of whatever race or persuasion could move about freely and with confidence, intermingling or not as they chose, being regarded and regarding each other as equals. How Carl Fields helped to bring this about during his years at Princeton, I shall leave it to his memoir to make clear.

While at the University of Zambia, Carl's talent and skill appear to have remained unflagging and to have produced impressive results there as well although directed toward a very different objective–the purposeful, systematic, forward-looking development of the nascent University as a whole. Yet, the social environment in which he found himself was radically different. He no longer stood out as a highly able black man operating in a largely white culture. He was now one more black man in a nation of blacks. He found, however, despite his color, his personality, and well-developed talents, as an American he was an outsider. As he wrote, "If you are not a Zambian, you're an expatriate. Color is not a factor."

The contrasts in these two phases of Carl Fields' life make reading this memoir a particularly interesting and rewarding experience. I commend it to potential readers for this reason, and also because it provides an introduction to an unusually gifted human being whose narrative style is lucid and non-pretentious.

Robert F. Goheen

August 2005 President, Princeton University, 1957-1972

TABLE OF CONTENTS

Princeton University

AFRICA

★University of Zambia

PREFACE

In the spring of 1964, Princeton University became the first predominantly white college in the United States to appoint a black administrator [Assistant Director of Student Aid]. Four years later, when I was appointed Assistant Dean of the College at Princeton, it made headlines around the world. In the fall of 1971, I was appointed Planning Officer of the University of Zambia, under the auspices of The Ford Foundation, a position that I held for three years. As it happened, I was the only black American planning officer in African university circles. The time between 1964 and 1974 has seen a great many changes take place in higher education and throughout the world. In one way or another, I have been a participant in or witness to some of these changes in higher education. It does seem that the experience of being the first black American administrator on both sides of the world, especially as a part of a black experience, would be of some use to others.

Everyone that I was in touch with was trying, in one way or another, to achieve something that would prove worthwhile to thousands of potentially capable students. The fact that, at times, they appeared more concerned with the preservation of institutions than they were with the development of new methods to improve opportunities for a formerly non-college-going population is part of the story of human development.

In order to keep the comparisons as clear as possible, I have put them down in the order in which they developed. In that way, I think the similarities and differences will be easier to ascertain and the systems made more understandable to the reader. I hope it will prove as interesting to read as it has been to live through being Black in Two Worlds

Carl A. Fields, January 1976

1

CHAPTER 1

HIRED—IVY LEAGUE STYLE

One Saturday morning during the Christmas holidays of 1963, I was in the third part of a deep sleep. My sons were in Brooklyn, so I was taking full advantage of the peace and quiet to sleep as long as possible. The phone began to ring. I let it sound off about seven or eight times, hoping it would prove to be a wrong number. Finally, I took the receiver off the hook and mumbled a drowsy hello.

A firm, wide-awake voice on the other end asked if he was speaking to Carl Fields. I answered in the affirmative. The voice went on to say that I had been hard to catch up with. I mumbled something about the fact that I was pretty busy and asked what I could do for him. The next words out of his mouth brought me fully awake. He wanted to know if I would be interested in an administrative position at Princeton University!

It wasn't uncommon for certain friends of mine or students whom I was counseling to call me at weird times of the day or night and ask all kinds of things, so I came fully alert trying to identify the voice. In the meantime, the voice on the other end must have sensed that I was about to hang up and asked me not to. He said he wasn't joking and identified himself as the representative of a well-known organization concerned with black educational advancement. That helped some. Yet I proceeded to ask him a series of questions aimed at trying to find out what he was up to.

"Where did you get my name?"

"From a contact in Alabama."

"Man, I don't know anybody in Alabama who would give you my name for a position at Princeton. No friend, that is."

"Just a minute," the voice said. "You know Bert Phillips, don't you?"

Sure, I knew Bert Phillips. We had worked together for three years while he was Director of Education at the New York Urban League. Then it clicked that Bert had taken the position of Dean of Students at Tuskegee. But why did this guy have to go all the way to Alabama to get my name?

It seems a friend of his, who was an administrator at Princeton, had called to ask his assistance. They were looking for a black man, with a certain kind of experience and background, to fill a new post. They had tried their own resources and had come up with a blank. Since he was in contact with a lot of black institutions, he'd been asked if he could possibly dig up someone for them. He was given the job specs and proceeded to call around to institutions that might have someone to fill the bill. In his telephone peregrinations, he had talked to Bert who told him that the person he knew was not in the South, but about a half hour away from his office in New York. Okay.

"You said Princeton, right?" I said, restraining myself from asking when Princeton had hired a black guy to do anything more than keep the grass cut or serve food to a bunch of well-to-do, southern-oriented students in a fancy club.

"There's been a change."

"When? How come I haven't heard of it before now?"

"Well, that's just the point. They don't want to make a big thing of it if there isn't going to be a pay off in terms of getting someone."

"Well, I've got a job and I don't think I'm interested."

The voice became a little more agitated.

"Look, I know how you must feel about Princeton, but I promised I'd come up with a name. Would you at least talk to somebody from there?"

"Okay, it won't hurt to talk, I guess."

"Thanks. How can they reach you?"

"I won't be in until after New Year's Day."

I gave him the phone number. After a few more amenities, he hung up, and I snuggled between the covers and promptly went back to sleep.

I didn't give any more thought to the subject until I returned to work and mentioned it to one of my colleagues. It really seemed to be part of a dream that I had had, and I was busy figuring out what that kind of dream was pointing to. My colleague, who was white, said he knew that Princeton was looking for someone. As a matter of fact, he had called to find out if the person had to be black and was told that was important. I asked how come he hadn't mentioned it to me. He said he didn't think I'd be interested. About that time my secretary came into the room and said there was a long-distance call for me.

I picked up the phone and a very quiet voice on the other end said, "I understand you are interested in an administrative position at Princeton."

I almost exploded as I answered, "You couldn't possibly have been told that. I was asked to talk to somebody about a position at Princeton. I don't know whether I'll be interested or not."

The voice hesitated a moment then said, "Yes, I believe that is the way it is. Would you talk to me about the position?"

I replied that I was pretty busy and time was hard to find. The voice insisted quietly that his time was my time–just name it–and he'd try to get to where I was. I decided not to be a boor and remembered my mother's injunction, "Always be nice to people; it doesn't hurt you. You can still do what you want to." I said, "All right," and we named a day and time.

On the day of the appointment, it began to rain in the morning and never stopped. I knew that nobody in his right mind would try to keep an appointment in such foul weather. I hung around the office until about fifteen minutes after the hour and then told my secretary that I was going off to see someone at the other end of the campus.* Just as I was about to leave, a thoroughly drenched man with a soaking wet umbrella and raincoat came through the door. I had seldom seen a person so wet. He took off his hat and rivulets of water ran to the floor.

"I'm looking for Mr. Carl Fields," he said. I said, "I'm he," and he stuck out his hand. "I'm Brad Craig from Princeton University."

I didn't know it then, but those six words were the beginning of a fine relationship and friendship with a very decent human being. As I helped him off with his raincoat and umbrella, I couldn't help saying to myself, "Damn! This guy must mean business." We went into my office. He took a seat and made himself as comfortable as he could in his condition. I wished that I had had a drink to give him. In a very quiet, deliberate voice, with frequent clearings of the throat, which I came to know as characteristic of him, Brad began to explain what he and Princeton were about.

I listened attentively for about fifteen minutes. When he came to a pause, I broke in and began the severest kind of interrogation I could muster. I forgot that he was wet–that he had shown up under really abominable conditions–and began to rake him and Princeton over the coals of black indignation. As it happened, I had personal understanding of the Princeton scene. A cousin of mine had tried to transfer there from Ohio State University in the middle 1930s.

---

* Fields was supervisor of counselor training at Teachers College, Columbia University.

He had a fine record at Ohio and was accepted on the face of that until he showed up for his interview. He was light enough to pass for white and things went well until he identified himself as the nephew of the leading black administrator in Trenton, New Jersey. At that point he was told that his application would be given consideration. He never got to Princeton as a student. He wound up working in one of the clubs on the campus. He used to regale us younger fellows with tales of the Princeton undergraduates. My grandfather used to drive past those forbidding gates every time he went to Princeton, and the picture of privilege and discrimination of that lily-white institution was burned into my mind. In my undergraduate years as a track athlete, I used to take particular pleasure in beating the best that that white institution could put out on the floor. But, at the same time, I had tremendous admiration for Bill Bonthron, one of the premier milers of the thirties. I had a real love-hate relationship from a distance.

After about three quarters of an hour of alternately questioning and haranguing, I cooled down and began to pay attention to the man and what he was saying. Princeton had come to a decision to appoint a black administrator. It had not been a hasty decision. The president of the university had led the effort to change the face of Princeton and open it up to any deserving student, black or white. The black students at the university were few, and some of those had not made it through the four years. They didn't know why. A black administrator might help shed some light on this and other problems. The position was in the Bureau of Student Aid, which Brad headed. The person appointed would be working with him. I didn't find out until later what an asset this would be. He put it plain and simple. He admitted to all that I had said about the place, but then asked if there wasn't room for change. He didn't know it, but he had touched a vulnerable spot. I came from a long line of Baptist-related people, ministers, et al., and the power of conversion was almost a given fact in my heritage.

We agreed that I would pay a visit to the university in order to meet some other people and take as much time as necessary to size up the situation. I suggested that I'd be down in about a month. Brad said that was too long and asked if I couldn't make it in two weeks. I got suspicious again and asked why. He said they wanted to fill the position for the next academic year. He then stated positively that, as far as he was concerned, I was the man for the position. He didn't want any slip-ups to occur. I agreed to the two-week date.

Between that interview and the time that I went to Princeton, I talked with and consulted all of the people who were close to me in the civil rights movement: colleagues, family, and even some people who I knew had no love for me personally but who respected me professionally. The sum total of their observations was, "You must be out of your mind to consider it." "Do you want to be cut off from the people?" "You ain't no Uncle Tom; what do you want to go there for?" "Forget it!" "You must be joking. All they want to do is say they had a black man under consideration, but he didn't meet their requirements." "Another putdown!"

My father looked at me and said, "It won't be the first time you've taken on something that looked impossible. If you think it will work, try it. Faith can overcome a lot of things that seem impossible." He was saying that out of a background of experience that we were both familiar with. When I was offered a scholarship, based on my athletic ability, to St. John's University, the Director of Athletics had stated quite candidly that this was the first time they were offering a full scholarship to a black (Negro) and that, if I made it, they would be encouraged to bring in more blacks (Negroes) under the same terms. My dad had looked at me then and said, "It's your decision." I took it! A hell of a way to start a college career, but it paid off.

On the day of the interview, I dressed with more than usual care in order to create the impression that I thought would set the tone for whatever was to happen. The importance of making a good first impression had been drummed into my head from childhood. My brothers and I never got out of the house without a final inspection by mama. "Look like what you are," she used to say. "You're a Fields, and that should mean something to you even if other people don't know it." Pride in family, pride in where you came from, pride in your heritage as a black person was built in years before the new black revolution sounded the slogan "Black is beautiful."

I hopped into my car, a 1963 Bonneville, black top with gray body, sat for a moment in silent prayer, and then started off: over the Cross Bronx Expressway, across the George Washington Bridge and onto the New Jersey Turnpike on the first of many trips over that route. I had considered the method of transportation carefully—train, bus or car—and had decided the car was the most feasible. If things didn't go well, I didn't want to be hanging around waiting for transportation back to the familiar environs of the city. If things did go well, I wanted to take off from there with all the aplomb I could muster. There's nothing like being able to get away from a good scene in a damn good car, with a wave of the hand or a nod of the head in farewell.

I like to drive. There's something about the purr of the motor that is conducive to in-depth thinking. Here I was on my way to what was called "the southernmost northern university in the East." I hadn't been in Princeton for years. Route 1 takes you right past the place. You have to have a special reason to turn off, and I'd never had a special reason until today. I tried to figure out whom I would see, what I should be looking for, what kind of tricky questions I would have to deal with. Should I play it cool, listen to what was said, and then get out? Face them with my knowledge of their discrimination against black people and tell them, "No thanks"? These thoughts were whirling through my head and before I knew it, I was off the New Jersey Turnpike at Exit 9, twenty minutes away from Old Nassau.

Down Route 1, right turn onto Washington Avenue, left turn onto Nassau Street and then another decision. Should I drive up to the gate, hoping that arrangements had been made for me to use the parking lot or park in a nearby lot and walk up to the building? I decided on the latter. No point risking possible insult by some guy who only followed orders. Better to walk through the gate like anybody else. Attract as little attention as possible. West College wasn't hard to find, and the directory on the inside wall told me where to find the Bureau of Student Aid. With a slightly faster heartbeat than usual, I took the steps two at a time and entered the office. The secretary was primed to expect a Mr. Fields and, with a welcoming smile, I was ushered into Brad Craig's office. A quick, firm handshake and the whole thing was underway.

I was given a general description of the work and responsibility of the Bureau and a rough description of what I would be expected to do if I accepted the position. Now I don't consider financial transactions and figuring to be my strong points. Right away I chalked up the fact that maybe this was one of the first signals that would set the stage for easing me out of consideration. Since the best defense is a good offense, I lost no time in stating that my experience in financial matters was limited. The response to that was an assurance that it wasn't that complicated and, with some briefing, I certainly would be able to handle things. Besides, I could always bring things to Brad if they proved to be too difficult. Signal No. 2? As long as you're black and take the job, we don't expect too much from you. Window dressing? Okay. Keep that in mind.

After about a half-hour of small talk about whether I had driven down or taken the train, Brad announced that we would be having lunch with a small group of people who had been active in supporting the idea of a black administrator. Ah ha! Now things would begin to shape up. So off we went to have lunch at the Nassau Inn. As we moved across the campus, we were joined by a couple of other men whose names I didn't immediately catch. I would have time for that later. Some more talk about how I'd got down there and where my car was. I told them I had parked outside the campus. Why? Orders had been left at the guard's kiosk to permit me to park inside. Oh? All right, someone had covered the small points to avoid discrimination.

The luncheon inside the dimly lit dining room of Nassau Inn was one of questions and answers. First, one of them, then me. I had mentally moved to the point of saying, "What the hell?" I had nothing to lose by stating where I was and what I thought, right out and as directly as I could. If they were going to accept me, it would be with complete awareness of what I stood for or not at all. They were all pleasant, and I could spot nothing that would lead me to believe that they were not sincere in their desire to have someone like me around. At the end of the luncheon, all expressed the hope that I would be joining them in the near future. I was noncommittal in my response, but that seemed to be all right.

The next stop was at the office of the Dean of the College, for another interview. Brad left nothing to chance. He waited with me until the dean was ready and introduced us. I was asked to stop by his office after the session with the dean and before I took my leave. The dean "looked" like Princeton. Tall, with mixed gray hair, a pleasant, intelligent, pensive face, he was wearing casually elegant tweeds that you knew damn well were expensive, but all low key. He asked some of the same questions that I had been asked before, and I gave back the same responses. He remarked about the variety and extent of my occupational background and said I didn't appear old enough to have done so much in such a short period of time.

It was about then that I began to feel that I was going to accept the job. I began to suspect that I would be really different from the usual person they hired for an administrative post. In order to make the kind of money that supports a reasonable life style, a black professional often has to take whatever he can as a job. For a period of about three to four years, I had worked three to four jobs at a time. Most of them were spin-offs of what I was doing during the day on a full-time basis. The hourly pay was good, and it was a needed supplement to full-time earnings. You didn't work like that because you wanted to make your résumé look good. That's for the birds. You worked, if you could, because you needed the bread.

Things were going along pretty well until the dean asked me a particular question. He wanted to know how I thought I would make out in dealing with "the sophisticated Princeton student." I asked him to explain what he meant. He stated that Princeton students were among the upper five percent of the most intelligent students in the country. They came from cultured backgrounds, some with an overlay of foreign travel and experience. Well, right then I almost told him what he could do with the job. Instead, I suggested that he might not have read my résumé too carefully. I had spent most of my life in New York City. I had met and worked with all kinds of people from all kinds of backgrounds and social status. Whatever I had not encountered in the way of sophistication probably didn't matter too much. I'd be perfectly content to let the Princeton students hold on to their brand of sophistication as long as it didn't interfere with what I was doing. If it did interfere, I would then decide how to handle it. I said all of this with a good bit of heat that the dean was quick to recognize. He immediately stated that he had not meant to imply that I would be over my head, but only wanted to alert me to the fact that Princeton was slightly different as a setting from what I might have encountered before.

The interview ended on a pleasant note, but I felt then that this man would have difficulty understanding what a person like me was all about. I walked slowly out of Nassau Hall with its smug aroma of history pervading the atmosphere and over to West College, no less smug in its ivy-covered setting. Was this really where I wanted to be, even for a short time? Could I stand all of this that reeked of a solid white American history of denial of the real worth or ability of the black as a fully functioning member of the society? What could a black man accomplish in this setting? I didn't mind taking on challenges, but this could be ridiculous!

Back in the Bureau office, I sat and talked plainly with Brad, letting some of what I had been thinking come into the open. He listened intently and finally said, "I would like to have you as a colleague. You're the man for this position. I don't think that you'll regret accepting it." Fair is fair! Brad was meeting me on equal ground and with equal openness. He didn't say it would be easy. He stated that I could handle it if I wanted to. We shook hands and I promised to let him know of my decision within two weeks.

The drive back to the city was as smooth as it had been on the way down to Princeton. My stay there had covered about two hours. Wrapped in the confines of my car, I thought over all that had taken place. Was this destiny of some sort? Why me out of all the well-qualified black men that I knew were around? God. It could be fantastic for a while. The irony of it began to appeal to me. Maybe some things could happen that would give Old Nassau some legitimacy to its colors of orange and black. Make the black on the flag a visible presence to be reckoned with.

By the time I reached the George Washington Bridge, I had begun to smile to myself and even laughed out loud a couple of times. I remembered two passages from the Bible relating to the reluctance of Moses to accept the responsibility of leading the children of Israel out of Egypt. On one occasion, he said, "I don't know what to say." God said, "Open your mouth, and I will speak for you." On another occasion he said, "I don't know which way to go." God said, "You take the first step, and I will do the rest." A saying from African literature came to mind: "The journey of a mile begins with a step." Now for sure I was no Moses, but I could take the first step. And I did.

CHAPTER 2

THE BLACK ADMINISTRATOR—A BEGINNING

Once I was certain that the job at Princeton was mine, I set up a carefully laid plan of orientation. Three to four months would elapse before I would actually take up my duties. In the meantime, I felt it necessary to get to know the place from as many points as possible. I arranged a schedule that would allow me to come down to Princeton about twice a week. Some time would be spent in the office reading material on the university, the Bureau, and all departments or divisions that it was in contact with. The other part of the time was spent roaming the campus, observing anything and everything: walking the streets of the town, watching people in stores and restaurants, taking advantage of the fact that nobody knew me or would pay any attention to a "tourist" in Princeton.

This was time well spent. I saw and heard much that was to come in handy in the future from the perspective of both town and gown. For instance, in 1964 you could find no black salesperson in any store or business on Nassau Street, yet there was a sizable black population that patronized all of the businesses in town. I found out that most of the black professionals living in Princeton practiced or worked outside of Princeton. The visible working black population was engaged in the same kinds of positions that they had held when I first saw the town as an elementary school student. On campus, the black student body was practically invisible. There were two black professors, neither of whom I saw nor talked to for the first two years I was there. The university appeared to be a well-oiled, smoothly efficient educational entity. In business for better than two hundred years, it had produced many of the men who had founded the country, housed the seat of national government, and produced presidents, statesmen, and business leaders who were part of the woof and warp of America. I had time to watch and observe it calmly and dispassionately.

I assumed official duties on the first of August 1964. Shortly thereafter, I was introduced to the president, Dr. Robert F. Goheen, who preferred to be called Bob. It was a short fifteen-minute contact with good wishes from him to me. I wasn't in his office again until the spring of 1967.

My duties were assigned, and I found, to my surprise, that I was to be part of the counseling group to freshmen and sophomores. I questioned this immediately. I was totally new to the Princeton system. I was told that the decision to put me into the counseling service was based on my past fifteen years of counseling experience. The mechanics of the system would be easy to master and any help that I needed with some of the more intricate questions or problems would be readily available. It was at this point that I threw the first curve ball. All right, I would serve as counselor, but I did not want any black students as counselees. What? But we thought that you would be interested in dealing with "our colored boys." Your error. I know how to deal with black people. If someone else has difficulty, let them look me up. Besides, I have my own way of getting to know them. It's important for me to know how you handle the people that you think or say you know. I was adamant on this point. If they wanted me to serve as counselor, there was no choice but to buy into my position. This was my first victory. A small one, but an important one. It set up a mutual rapprochement. I'll play your game, if you play mine.

For the rest of the first few weeks of the academic term, I often wished that I had had a candid camera crew at my disposal. The offices of the Bureau were being redecorated, and I was assigned an office at the rear of the floor. John Danielson, who later became and remained one of my closest friends, occupied the front office. I had looked over the list of names of the students assigned to me and where they were from. Two-thirds of them were from below the Mason-Dixon Line. I knew what was going to happen. None of those kids had had to ask a black man for anything during his life. Now they were going to be confronted with a black who could say yes or no to anything they had in mind and control, up to a point, the beginning of their academic careers at Princeton. It was a gas.

I had placed my desk at the opposite corner of the room from the door. In order to get to me, they had to enter through John's office. I sat and waited. "Good morning, sir. Are you Mr. Fields?" "No, Mr. Fields is in the next office." "Thank you, sir." There would be a polite knock on the door. I'd say, "Come in." The door would open and into the room would step a fresh, apple-cheeked youngster, correct as could be. I would rise from my chair, stick out my hand and say, "I'm Mr. Fields." Talk about culture shock. There would be hesitation, a look at his card to see if he had the right name, a surprised expression and a quick recovery. The whole process took him less than ten seconds, but I'm sure that it was the longest ten seconds that he had lived through up to that point.

I would carry on as though it was the most natural thing in the world for this boy from the South to expect to be dealt with by a black professional at Princeton. Having taken care of business, I would direct him to the next point and make an appointment to see him again within a couple of weeks. In the meantime, he was informed that if something arose before then he could feel free to make his own appointment to see me. Another handshake and out the door he would go.

The second time around was as interesting. By then they knew I was black. I knew that in the interim they had checked out their other friends or older students to find out if they too had a black counselor. They came in more composed but still a little unsure of what to expect. I would then tell them that I knew it was a little unusual for them to find a black administrator as their counselor at Princeton. I was interested in seeing to it that they got the best service possible. If they felt strained or awkward in talking to me about their academic problems, I would understand, and they had the option of selecting another person on the counseling staff. I would even recommend someone if they were not familiar with the other persons. Not one student took me up on that suggestion during the whole time I was part of the counseling service. It was an interesting look at a new and young America.

I have already mentioned that I had decided not to be thrust onto the black student body in an official position. I ascertained exactly how many were on the campus—twelve undergraduates and four graduate students. Most of the undergraduates were in the freshman class, so, in a sense, we were starting out together. I took advantage of the time that I had created and observed their behavior and actions as Princeton students. It was painful. There were never more than one or two together at any time on the campus. They usually in the company of several white students going to class or lunch or dinner. I don't think that any of them were together in the same classes or tutorial groups. The emphasis was supposed to be on integration of the black student into the Princeton body. There were even a couple of students who were light enough to pass.

It was about three months after I had begun work at Princeton before a black student spoke to me. It caught me by surprise. Badi

Foster, a graduate student, had seen me approaching his table in the cafeteria and asked me if I would join him. I did. He questioned me as to my status, and I told him that I was an administrator in the Bureau of Student Aid. He was surprised and almost unbelieving. Badi had spent most of his childhood in Morocco.* He had come to the United States as a scholarship student at the University of Denver and then on to Princeton. He was as unprepared as were the southern white students to meet a black at Princeton in an administrative capacity. He said that he would drop by my office and chat, and I said that would be fine.

About a week later, I staged my own encounter with another black student, Jerry Ingram. I knew him because he was on the football team and great things were expected of him. I stopped him as he was leaving the student cafeteria, introduced myself and my position, and asked him why blacks on campus seemed to avoid each other and certainly made no attempt to find out who strangers were. He was nonplussed. I asked him to give the other fellows a message from me. I said that I expected to be spoken to if they were within hailing distance. If they didn't recognize me, I would leave no doubt in their minds as to how I would recognize them–and in their own language. He said, "Yes, sir, I'll tell them." I waited to see what would happen.

Several days later I was coming from the parking lot during a class change. I spotted a black student coming toward me in the company of three white students. I fixed my eyes on him, and, as we came closer, looked at him with a smile of recognition. He quickly said, "Hello, sir," and hurried by. But that had broken the ice. The next afternoon during lunch break, I placed myself on the campus outside of West College and waited for someone to come by. Most of the students used the short cut across the campus that

---

* His parents, Ruth and Bill Foster, were Baha'i missionaries there.

passed in front of the building. Again I saw a black student in the company of white students coming my way. This time I called him and said I'd like to speak to him. His companions hesitated, looked at me curiously and then proceeded on their way. He was obviously discomfited, but polite. I engaged him in some conversation for about two minutes and shortly, along came two more black students. I stopped them too. In a matter of about five minutes we formed a small group of six blacks, standing together outside of West College and Nassau Hall. That was the first of many similar meetings in the same spot. A little coercion at first to get things off the ground, but from that point on it became a mutual-assistance group on all fronts.

Meanwhile, administratively, things were moving along. I was learning the basic routines with lots of assistance from Brad and John. Other colleagues joined us for lunch and, through informal conversations, a friendly atmosphere was built up. It was close to the end of the first year when the second incident occurred that was going to help define my role as a black administrator. I was sent for by the Dean of the College who said that there was a problem that he hoped I could help with. Three black students were in danger of flunking out, one freshman and two sophomores. One of the sophomores was the other black student on the football team (whom I hadn't met) and had been slated for a starting position the next year. An average student in his freshman year, he had slumped badly in the second half of his second year, and no one could find out why. He had refused to disclose anything of consequence, even to the football coaches. This was really bad news. The other two had suddenly seemed to stop functioning after good beginnings. When they had been told of the possibility of dismissal for failing performance, they had accused the officials of inadequate assistance and a poor climate within which to carry on successful study. Although they did not use the words, the implication was discrimination. Again, repeated efforts on the part of other administrators had elicited no further information of consequence. This was a potentially harmful situation to an administration that was trying cautiously and carefully to introduce a change of image into the academic and social community from which it drew its student body. I agreed to see the students, if they wanted to see me. In each case, the student agreed to come and see me, and we began to get things cleared up. The sophomore football player had been quietly married for about a year. His wife was pregnant. She was living with relatives about fifty miles away from Princeton. He had been spending weekends with her, and this had cut study time. The regulations required a student to inform the authorities of an impending marriage. Since this was an all-male campus and there were no provisions for undergraduate married housing, the student was faced with a support problem. If he was on scholarship or financial aid, the provisions covered him only. A few students had left school because of their inability to take care of both home and study responsibilities. The footballer was in a dilemma and had not felt that the coaches or other authorities would understand or wish to help if they knew his circumstances.

The other two failing students had come from strong black community and family settings. They felt that Princeton offered them nothing in the way of personal definition aside from the status of students. They spent more time worrying about how to resolve the social situational scene than on study. Eventually, they were both succumbing to the alienation of the Princeton setting. Why hadn't they talked about this to anyone else? "Do you think a white man would know what we were talking about?"

All three cases called for policy decisions. Although not very big ones, they were important ones to the black student community. The footballer was given permission to bring his wife down, and housing was arranged in the graduate student housing area. In

addition, his financial aid was adjusted to cover rent and expenses.
The two failing students were given permission to continue study
at a recognized institution of their choice. Pending the result of
their academic grades, they would be accepted back at Princeton in
order to continue their academic careers.

A major point had been made. The normal Princeton scene was
inimical to the interests of and progress of the black student.
Something would have to be done. Ideas anyone? Not a clue.
Several white student counselees also encountered difficulties of the
same nature as far as alienation from the Princeton scene was
concerned. More ammunition for change.

By the beginning of the next academic year, I had decided that
it was time for me to get to know, if I could, the black community
in Princeton. This was not as simple as it sounds. I knew one
person, a retired Baptist minister, who had been a close friend of
my grandfather. He hadn't seen me in years. I paid him a visit, but
it was obvious that he would not be able to help even though I
could use his name as a reference. Where to begin? It was then that
I began to realize that being black and situated at Princeton in an
administrative position could become a liability if I didn't play
things right. Why? Because at that point in time, most black
communities had developed their own values and measures that
were applied rigorously to situations they were familiar with. To be
hired as a professor in an all-white institution was one thing. It
proved that you were as good in your field as they were. You did
your thing the way you wanted to in the classroom, and you might
even publish a book or two. More power to you for breaking
through. To be an administrator, a part of the system that had
"done things" to you or people that you knew, was quite something
else. I knew that from my own community in Bedford Stuyvesant
and other places that I had been in contact with.

The cleaning crew for my building was all black. So were most of the crews in other buildings on campus. This was their turf. The man assigned to the second floor was called Jim. I knew that he had paid attention to me and knew as much as possible about the new face in West College. We had spoken to each other politely for more than a year. He was busy with his work and, at the time he came in, I was making tracks out of there back to the Bronx. I had, however, been watching him pretty closely and finally decided that he was the person to whom I would make my pitch.

I stayed behind purposely one day, beyond the five o'clock whistle. When Jim came back to my office, he was surprised to see me, but greeted me as usual and started for the waste paper basket beside my desk. I moved to the door and closed it. He heard the click and turned to me with an inquiring look. I asked him if he would mind taking time out for a while and answer some questions. He said, "Okay." I began by asking him what his last name was. His eyes opened a little wider. "Why?" he responded. "Well, everybody has a last name and I'd like to know yours. If my wife or friends came down and I met you on the street, I'd like to introduce you as 'Mr. Somebody.'" He said he had been working in that building for five years and that this was the first time that anyone had asked him his last name. I retorted that this was the first time a black man had been in an official position in this building, and I was different. He broke into a grin and said, "My last name is Butts." I walked over to him and shook hands. "Glad to know you, Mr. Butts." He asked me if he could smoke and I said, "Pull up a chair." He sat down and we began to talk. I told him that I wanted to get to know the black community. He asked me why. I said, "Because I'm black, too." He said that he knew that, but I didn't need the black community because I had it made with my job. I responded that one man never had it made if he had to depend only on himself. I needed cohorts. Black cohorts. I needed them from the community, and I thought he could help me. He studied me intently for a long minute. He then said, "I've been watching you and I've talked to some of my friends about you. You appear to be different from some people I know in good positions. Let me think about this for a while. I'll get back to you." I said that was all right with me. We smiled at each other—two black men, Mr. Butts and Mr. Fields.

About two weeks went by. I saw him several times, but all we said was "Hello" and each of us kept going. At the beginning of the third week, I decided to take the bull by the horns again. I stopped him this time as I was going out of the door. "Any word yet on how I make it?" He smiled and said, "I was trying to figure out if you were serious or just making conversation." "I know," I replied. "Man, I'm serious. Dead serious." He then asked me where I ate lunch. I told him at different places. He asked if I had ever been to the restaurant down Witherspoon Street, the Steak House. I said I hadn't. He suggested that I go in there for lunch one day and the maitre d' would pick me up. He was another black man, and he had been told to watch out for me. "Do I need a name?" I asked. "No," he said. "I've described you, and he'll be watching for you." "Thanks," I said.

The next day I couldn't wait for lunchtime to arrive. I turned down about three invitations to eat with some of the fellows in the building and hied myself off to the Steak House. I walked to the rear entrance as I had been instructed, opened the door and stood inside. A light-skinned, black man in waiter's uniform looked at me and said that there was no room there, please go to the front entrance. I hesitated a moment, then thanked him and headed for the front entrance. As I opened the door, the phone was ringing. The maitre d' looked up as I stood waiting, said, "Okay, Ernie," and came towards me. "I was told to send you back to the rear entrance." I turned and went back to the door. As I opened it the same man was standing there. "Is your name Fields? Do you work at the University?" "Yes," I replied, "To both questions." "There are no tables. Do you mind sitting at the counter?" "No, that's fine." "Good. That way I'll have more of a chance to talk to you." That he did for the next forty-five minutes. Where was I from? How long had I been at the university? Unbelievable! He had checked this out with some people who were supposed to be in the know. They knew nothing about me. "I know," I responded. He remembered seeing the announcement in the paper about a man being appointed who had been with the Urban League, but there had been no picture. "I know." Did I ever come down on football weekends? "Yes." Was I coming down for the big homecoming game? I could. Why? There's another black man who works the big days and if I were coming he'd alert him to look out for me too. "You can bet on it. I'll be down." "Fine." "Good to know you." "Come in again." "Soon."

I finished eating, left a good tip, shook hands and went back to the office feeling good. Chalk one up for me.

CHAPTER 3

BLACK UP CLOSE

I sat in the living room of the first black home to which I had been invited. It was attractively furnished. I went over in my mind the sequence of events that had led up to the invitation. After the football game the weekend before, I had gone as directed to the restaurant where I had had lunch. The place was crowded, but I noticed that there were no black people waiting for tables. The maitre d' had seen me the moment I entered the door. He gave me one sharp look and proceeded to take care of people who were ahead of me. When they were seated, he came to me. He was a man of medium height, moustache shaped just right on a pleasant, brown-skinned face. His black suit was well cut and gave him just the right appearance. His voice was well modulated and smooth as he asked me how many there were with me. I said two, my wife and me. He was looking me over and, at the same time, keeping his eye on what was going on in the restaurant.

I waited for the question to be asked as to my identity. It came. Was I Mr. Fields? I nodded in assent. The "passing on" process was still working. He identified himself as Floyd Campbell. We shook hands. He said there were no tables for two, but if I would wait out in the courtyard, he'd see to it that we got drinks, and he would call us as soon as there was a vacancy. That would be fine, I stated, and went out into the courtyard. In a few moments, a waiter appeared, took our order and returned with the drinks. We sat there watching the ebb and flow of people who were trying to get into the restaurant. Quite a few decided not to wait. Others took tables and ordered drinks. I looked up and saw another black couple moving toward the door. They went inside, but in a few minutes came back out, escorted by Floyd. As they headed toward our table, I rose in preparation for an introduction. Floyd made the introductions and then asked if we had any objections to sharing a table with the new arrivals. It was easier to get a table for four than for two. We all agreed, and Floyd went off to order drinks for Dr. and Mrs. Peterson. They were a friendly, affable couple. Who was I? What was I doing at Princeton? When I told them, they looked at each other with raised eyebrows. How long had I been there? How come nobody knew me? I explained again the events of my appointment and why no one knew that I was black.

Mrs. Peterson shrugged her shoulders and said that was typical of Princeton. By the time we had been seated and ordered our food, we were on a first-name basis, and the questions were coming thick and fast. What did I think I could do at Princeton? I launched into a recital of what I had in mind that I was to repeat over and over in the months to come. The need to establish a black presence on the campus. The need to find a way by which the black students who were there and those who were to come would have a more congenial atmosphere in which to study and be people in their own right. The need to establish firm ties with the black community in order to engender the support that I felt would be one of the key elements in their adjustment to Princeton. The need for me to meet and discuss what could be done by the black community in this respect.

By the end of dinner I had two converts and names of other

people who might be interested. Chet and Burnetta Peterson hoped that I would be successful, but they doubted that I could make a dent in the armor of the Princeton hierarchy. It just wasn't in the cards for them to let a black man, no matter how capable, change the pattern of things. Still, they wished me luck and asked to be kept informed about what I was doing. I said that I would. They gave us an open invitation to call on them any time we were in town. When the bill came, Chet asked if I would mind him taking care of it in a spontaneous gesture of acceptance of us. He rose and walked over to Floyd, and they exchanged a few words, looking in my direction. As we joined them at the door, Floyd asked me to call him during the week to make a date to have dinner at his home. I agreed.

The appointment had been for a Thursday evening at seven. I was there and now I would see what this opportunity would bring. Floyd came into the room followed by an attractive, light-skinned black woman with a friendly face. This was Mrs. Campbell, or Connie as I was to know her. Floyd left to get me a scotch and water, and Connie excused herself to go back to the preparation of dinner. The drinks were brought in, we toasted each other and then Floyd dropped the bombshell. He was very sorry, but he could not stay for dinner. He was Grand Master of the Masonic Lodge (black branch) in Princeton, and an emergency meeting had come to his attention. He might be back before I left, but if not he would see me again soon. I stood there looking at him with a frozen smile, my mind whirling like mad. What the hell kind of business was this, I asked myself. Had I done something wrong? Had he found out something that made him leery of wanting to know more about what was going on? Had Chet said something to him that was unfavorable? These and a hundred more questions flashed through my head in a few seconds. I finally said that I understood. It was all right. I'd talk to his wife, and she could explain things to him. He excused himself and went upstairs to get dressed. On the way, he informed Connie that he would not be staying for dinner. I could tell by the tone of her voice that she was as surprised as I was. She came into the room and began to explain the duties of a Grand Master and how disruptive things could get at times. I realized that she was trying to cover up, and I told her that I understood those things.

In a few minutes, Floyd returned to the room, all dressed except for his jacket. He said that he had a few minutes before had had to leave, and asked if he could freshen my drink. He came back with one of his own and then asked me what I wanted to talk with them about. I looked at him closely for a moment. What was this dude up to? Okay. I'd try to give him a thumbnail sketch. I began to talk rapidly in short, descriptive sentences about what I had observed on the campus. After a few minutes, I saw by his expression that he had begun to get interested in what I was saying…not just polite, but interested. Ah ha, I said to myself, I've got him hooked. If I can help it, he isn't going to any meeting tonight.

A half hour later, we were eating dinner, and I was still talking. Finally, at about ten o'clock, I remarked that I was sorry that I had caused him to miss the meeting. I'd resume talking with him at a later date. He asked me if I had to rush off. I said no. By midnight I was beginning to feel the strain that I had been under for the past four and a half hours, but it had not been in vain. Both Floyd and Connie were enthusiastic, and they would see to it that my story got around. They began to discuss between them the next person that I should see. We had begun to form a trio that eventually would get things off the ground. I was overjoyed. I had cut through. I wasn't alone anymore. If it could work for me, it could work for the students as well.

Connie called a few days later and told me to go to the YWCA and see a Mrs. Susie Waxwood. She was black and the first woman

30   BLACK IN TWO WORLDS

of their color to head the YWCA. Both she and her husband were
very influential in the white and black community.* If I could sell
her on my idea for community involvement, I'd be way ahead of
the game. I thanked her and placed a call to the YWCA as soon as
she hung up. The next day I was at the Y seated in an outer office
waiting to talk to Mrs. Waxwood. Susie Waxwood was a pleasant,
matronly looking woman with a frank, open countenance. She
wore glasses and talked rapidly in a soft voice with just a trace of
southern drawl. She had been filled in by Connie, but wanted to
hear from me what I thought the community could do. I went
through my story again. At the end of the hour, she said she would
help me in every way she could. If I wanted to meet and talk with
people, she would see to it that I got the opportunity. She would
take care of making the contacts. I should hold myself in readiness
for her call. She was warm, motherly, efficient, and she made me
feel good. I left there with my head in the clouds and singing a song
of thanks to Jim, the janitor at West College, and Ernie, the waiter
at the Steak House.

The weeks that followed were hectic and interesting. I met
people. I talked to people. I answered questions by the dozen. I
hardly knew what home looked like. But finally we, the
community and I, had put together a plan. I would get the names
of the incoming black students as soon as possible before the
beginning of the academic year.

Each family would select a student to sponsor in the community in any way it saw fit. I would write to the students explaining the

---

* Mrs. Waxwood's husband, Howard B. Waxwood, Jr., was principal of the Witherspoon School, an elementary school for Colored children, from 1936 to 1948. He later
became principal of John Witherspoon School (1948-1968), the junior high school
(grades 6-8) when the Princeton Plan that desegregated the public schools was adopted
following a court order in 1947 by the State of New Jersey that determined that school
segregation was unconstitutional.

program and telling them it was a voluntary effort on the part of the community to see to it that they had a home away from home. I would also send a letter to the parents of the incoming students informing them of this effort on the part of the University and the community. The students would be contacted by the family sponsors either before they arrived or as soon after as possible. It was simple but wholeheartedly backed by the black community.

Before the end of that academic year, I had written a proposal in which I had extended this idea to include selected white students as well as black in the family-sponsor plan. I showed it to Brad who was very interested and said that he would pass it along to the dean. I was informed a week later that I had been invited to present the proposal to an administrative committee headed by the dean. This committee would approve or disapprove the proposal depending upon how they saw the need for such action. I got a run-down from Brad on the composition of the committee–who was liberal and who was conservative. This was the next test of the role of the black administrator. It was again a policy decision that would affect not only the lives of the black students, but mine as well, as far as Princeton was concerned.

I had already reached a decision as to how I was going to handle the Princeton situation. If anyone asked me how long I was going to be there, I would tell them that it was a year-to-year proposition. If things were going well, I'd continue. If they weren't, I'd leave. I had found out that the majority of administrators, and a good many faculty people, felt that being at Princeton was almost like making it to heaven. They were really tied into the place. I felt that I had to take a different tone if I were to register as my own kind of man on that campus. It was always interesting to see the questioning stare or the disbelief that registered on the faces of people when I would say that one year at Princeton was all that I needed to make it possible for me to go anywhere I wished. With that on my résumé, I almost had carte blanche into any other situation. When they asked how I came to that conclusion, I would ask them how many other black administrators did they know of who could claim Princeton as their last place of employment. It worked every time!

The committee meeting was held in the dean's office in Nassau Hall. It was my first official attendance at any committee meeting. I was tuned to a high pitch, ready for anything that came down the pike. With Brad at my side, I arrived a few minutes early and took a seat where I was sure that I could see everyone in the room. Everyone was relaxed and friendly in his greeting. That's the Princeton way. I don't care how important the issue might be; at the beginning of things, everyone is relaxed and informal. It can be very deceptive to the newcomer. Once the meeting gets underway, you better damn well know which end is up or you're in real trouble.

My proposal was the last item on the agenda. I sat through what was to me a lot of meaningless talk. All my thoughts were on the proposal and how I would handle it. Finally, it was my turn, and the dean, after a few introductory remarks, put me on. They all had copies of the proposal, so I was brief and to the point in expanding on what I considered to be the necessity for such a program. I referred to my experience as a counselor for freshman students and the observations that I had made as to the effect of the Princeton climate on those who had come from a different milieu. I trotted out the socio-psychological implications of alienation on students and the reasons why Princeton should take cognizance of this phenomenon. It took about fifteen minutes.

There was a short period of silence and then the questions and statements began to come. Direct, hard, searching. Didn't this sound like an attempt to spoon feed and mollycoodle the Princeton student? How could I be so sure of my assumptions about the

Princeton student? I hadn't been around long enough to know what I was talking about. Where would I get these family sponsors from? Maybe I could depend on the white community, but where did I get the idea that I could get anything from the black community?

I responded to the questions and the statements in calm, measured tones and words. I reminded those who did not know that I was a trained observer of human behavior with fifteen years of experience behind me. The Princeton student was no different from any other person when he was in emotional or mental conflict. I had been a member of the counseling unit for almost two years. I had had ample time to talk with and find out about most of the students that were part of my caseload. I had discussed my observations with a few other people who had been on the campus longer than I, and they shared my views that something should be done to try to make the problems of adjustment to Princeton easier.

Then the attack on the proposal became more direct and, at the same time, more subtle. What about the black student at Princeton? Was I trying to imply that he was not capable of keeping up academically? They had tried to select the best available. If there were complaints about the way they were treated, why hadn't this come to the attention of authorities before now? What made me think that I understood the problems of blacks better than anyone else in the room? A Princeton student was a Princeton student, not white or black! He was selected from among the upper five percent of outstanding students across the country. One member voiced the hope that my proposal would not go beyond the walls of that room.

In spite of myself, I exploded. I told them that I had every right to speak for the black students because I was a black man. I knew about the situation they were living through because I had had a similar experience during my own college days. No, they would not be aware of the feelings of the black students because no one could voice them for fear that he would be considered trying to cop out from academic rigor. I stated flatly and unequivocally that no one in the room had more knowledge about the black student than I did, and if they thought they did, they were under an illusion. There were black families of substance in the community, and they were as interested in assisting the black students as much as white families were interested in assisting their own kind. I didn't wonder that they had no real knowledge of the black community because they probably had made little or no attempt to find out about those "good colored people" down Witherspoon Street.

As I finished the blast, I looked over at Brad. He had a grim expression on his face. I said to myself, "Okay man, you've blown it." But I couldn't have cared less at that moment. The Petersons had been right. I had been right in my earlier misgivings about taking the job. They were not interested in changing a damn thing. Well, they could shove it. I'd start looking for another job as soon as possible

Then, into the silence of the room that was thick with repressed feelings of anger and frustration came the quiet voice of Dean Douglas Brown. He was Dean of Faculty, a beloved and respected man as a teacher and as a person. He had years of experience in government and academic circles and was the reputed father of the national social security system. He was almost at the end of a distinguished career at Princeton.

He said that he had listened with great interest to the discussion and had read the proposal carefully. In his time he had seen a lot of Princeton students, and there was some truth to the allegation that I had made about the lack of adjustment that some experienced. He stated with a smile that he had good friends in the black community, but that he might not know as much about the community as he should. He felt that maybe I should hold off my efforts to take on too many students, but that the proposal had merit, and he, for one, would approve giving me the green light to try it out and report back to the committee at the end of the year what the results of the program had been.

The voice of Doug Brown was like the voice of the president. It carried weight. The atmosphere in the room suddenly became lighter. The dean said that he did not feel that white students needed the program, but if I wanted to pursue it with the black students, I could. He cautioned me to keep them informed about the progress of the program and not to hesitate to give up on it if it didn't work.

The meeting was adjourned. The men filed out of the room, some with a nod of the head in my direction, some with faint smiles, but I could sense no real hostility. Maybe a shade more respect for my having stood firm and stated my case in a positive manner against a wave of negative reaction.

I walked over to Dean Brown with an outstretched hand and thanked him for his support. He looked at me with a twinkle in his eye as he filled his pipe and said, "Well, I believe in giving a fellow a chance. We would not be where we are today if somebody hadn't taken a chance on something new. Do the best you can and good luck to you."

I smiled back. He had read my thoughts accurately. Brad gave me a firm handclasp, and we walked out of the room and over to our offices. He said that I had gained a valuable ally in Dean Brown and that he was sure that I would have no interference with the plan. He said that he would do all he could to assist the program in getting off the ground. I nodded and went into my office, closed the door and sank slowly into my chair. Another round won, and I was still on the move. God surely was smiling in my direction. I murmured a silent prayer of thanks.

Two or three weeks later I was asked to join President Goheen at lunch in the cafeteria. He had heard about the Family Sponsor Plan and wanted to talk with me about it. I explained the rationale behind the plan. He said it was difficult for him to understand the situation as it affected black students. He also questioned whether there were enough black families in the area to support and give assistance to "educated" black students at Princeton. I said that there were, and it was unfortunate that the Princeton academic community didn't know more about the people right in their own back yard. The fact of the matter was that the black community was just about as invisible as it could get in the eyes of most of the white population; there, but not there, unless it was a question of getting votes or pushing through a bond issue for property holders.

The summer was filled with feverish activity, getting the details of the program settled, writing letters, and doing the hundred other things that always accompany a new venture. Finally, everything was in place but one item. During Freshman Week, students were moved around the campus from one meeting to another. It was a general orientation to the ins and outs of the campus and to who was who. With the inception of this program, I felt that it was time for me to come out of the cocoon and appear as what I was, the black administrator of Princeton.

I stated that I wanted to have a meeting with all of the black freshmen, with refreshments and all the other amenities that were common to special groups on campus. I was prepared for a negative reaction, and I got it. Wouldn't it look strange for the black students to be singled out for special meetings? No. Wouldn't they think that Princeton was being discriminatory right from the beginning? No. Why couldn't I have other, white administrators at the meeting? Because it was my idea and my meeting. Permission was finally given, albeit reluctantly. Chalk up another one for me!

That first meeting was memorable and historic in the life of the

black campus community. I had asked some of the black sophomores and juniors to be there to welcome their brothers. They were
there. This was the largest group of blacks to come into a class at
that time, about fourteen of them. They came in ones and twos,
until finally the whole group was assembled. I introduced myself.
There was visible astonishment on the faces of quite a few of them.
A black administrator at Princeton? How come? How long?

They were filled in on the details and then on the reasons for the
Family Sponsor Program. Some of them had already been in touch
with their families and the others had made arrangements to be
picked up or make the first visit. I told them that, at the end of the
week, there would be a party for old and new black students at the
home of one of the black families. They all said they would be
there.

The affair was held at the home of Jim and Fanny Floyd. Their
older son, Jim, Jr., had been admitted to Princeton in the Class of
1969. He was the first, native born, black Princetonian to be
admitted to the university in about twenty years. His maternal
grandfather had been a head steward at one of the eating clubs for
thirty years. When he retired, members of the club came from all
over the United States to pay tribute to him. One of the first things
I had been shown when I hit the campus was the picture of this
beloved and respected gentleman, prominently displayed in the
foyer of the club. Princeton's touch of democracy.

I kept the picture showing all of the black students of the
university sitting around the basement playroom of Jim Floyd's
house. I knew that things would never be the same again for any
black student entering Old Nassau! One year later, the result of the
program spoke for itself. All of the entering freshmen had passed
and were now sophomores. It had never happened before. The
failure rate among black newcomers to the university had been
about 50 percent. The black community had come through with a

bang. The whole administration knew that Fields' plan had produced amazing results. I was there for another year.

CHAPTER 4

CRISIS IN BLACK

The academic year 1966-67 was to mark the coming of age of the black presence on the Princeton campus. By September of 1966, there were forty-one undergraduates, all shades and sizes of young black men. The incoming black freshmen were now being greeted by an enthusiastic group of black students and black community people. Black parents, who accompanied their sons to school, were pleasantly surprised to find out that they didn't have to rush off because there were no rooms available around Princeton. They had accommodations in black homes. It was beginning to be a common sight to see groups of three or more black students walking across the campus, deep in conversation or laughing and joking–more relaxed, more self-assured.

My office had by now become the unofficial headquarters and meeting place for the black students. I was still counselor to freshman and sophomore students, and I still had an all-white group. There was a slight difference. No longer did the white student, new to the campus, greet me with a shocked expression on his face. Instead, there was a ready smile and a sense of expectancy that something interesting could take place. Several of my white counselees had been saved from flunking out, and the word was out about the fact that I could be helpful. The consequent traffic pattern back and forth to my office was probably the most interesting mixture of black and white on campus.

By the time the football season was half over, I began to sense that the black students were beginning to think of coming together in a more organized fashion. I was well aware that the trend of organized groupings of black students had begun in some of the other Ivy League institutions. As a matter of fact, I had attended a couple of "Soul" meetings that had been held at Yale and Harvard. I believe I'm correct in stating that the impetus for this movement originated with a group of black students from the South who had been members of the Student Non-Violent Coordinating Committee (SNCC). They were veterans of sit-ins, marches, and jail confinements. Their brand of organizing didn't quite get off the ground, but it gave birth to the movement that saw black student organizations of all kinds become a part of every predominantly white campus in the country.

I was for organization, but not just any kind. In my mind, it had to have form and purpose that would not only bring it visibility, but create an effective force for positive change on the campus. As a result, long hours of conversation and discussion in my office and in students' rooms took place over a period of three to four months. I know that at times they thought that I was being an obstructionist, maybe even a little bit of an Uncle Tom. But I had seen a lot of good-intentioned organizations go down the drain for lack of soundly developed and thought-out goals and purposes. If I could help it, that was not going to happen on this campus. Timing and readiness were two important words to me, and I knew the significance of both to Princeton. From my off-hand probing of my colleagues, I knew that the students were not ready. So I waited for God to smile on me, and He did.

The Governor of Alabama, George Wallace, had begun an early

and active campaign that he hoped would land him in the White House. His itinerary included many college campuses, and his reception by groups of "radical" and black students on these campuses had furnished a lot of newsprint for Mr. Wallace. A very astute politician, he knew a good thing when he saw it and made capital of the reaction of students as often as possible. We found out that he had been invited to speak at Princeton by one of the oldest student societies on campus, Whig-Clio. This was a debating society and, over the years, many controversial people and topics had been aired on the campus. It was natural, therefore, for the society to conclude that a person as controversial as George Wallace would carry on the purpose of the society and the academic community as a forum for reasoned debate on his candidacy for president of the United States.

The reaction to his coming was loud and swift throughout the campus. As one would expect, the campus was split into two broad groups: one advocating his right to be heard in conformance with democratic tradition, the other stating categorically that they already knew what he had to say, and he did not need to repeat it at Princeton. I got wind of the fact that a group of students had invited some of the senior blacks to a meeting to discuss ways and means of developing a demonstration aimed at disrupting whatever Mr. Wallace was going to do or say. I checked to find out who the organizers were and ascertained that they were among the liberal but radical-left students on campus. This was serious.

I had met quite a few students and faculty who had participated in some of the protest marches in the South. They were honest and sincere advocates of freedom for all. But I must admit that I had seen little evidence that they had registered any impact on Princeton, either in the community or on campus. They considered themselves the exponents of the "Negro" cause, but this was the time, I reasoned, for blacks to speak for themselves. We were visibly among them, but they didn't see us. It was a situation that had its counterparts in many areas of the North.

I contacted the organizer of the meeting and told him that I wanted to attend. He seemed a little surprised but said that it was all right. I then called the two men who were going to represent the black students and suggested that they not accept any proposal at the meeting. I emphasized the fact that we would have to wait and see if the tactics or plans devised were ones we could see ourselves carrying out. If not, we would have to discuss the proposals among ourselves. They concurred. I knew what was going to happen but felt that the students would have to have their own experience.

During my tenure as Director of Education for the Urban League of Greater New York, I had acted as coordinator of a combined group of civil rights organizations, black and white. For years, some of the white groups had been in the forefront of the fight for equal rights for blacks and had had good success in their undertakings. It came as a shock, in one crucial situation involving the struggle for school integration, when the black caucus of this group decided that they would take the lead in stating their case and how it should be handled. The black caucus made its point over the protestations of the white members who failed to understand that the time had come when blacks had to speak for themselves as principals, not as bystanders. The group was never the same.

The meeting on the campus involved about fifteen people of student and faculty status. The organizers began to describe their plan of action. It was not new. Placards denouncing Mr. Wallace, attempts at confrontation, planned interruption of his speech; they had all been used before, and Mr. Wallace had always come out on top.

After the explanation, I suggested that this was not the best way to deal with the situation, and that it certainly would not help the cause of black students on the campus to be involved in proceedings that could result in a fracas with the local police and state troopers. The organizers listened politely but rejected my suggestions on the grounds that blacks on the campus had not had the experience that they had in handling situations of this kind and that they might be guided by those who had. This was what I had expected. The black student representatives were first amazed, then angry at the inference of their inadequacy. They stated their opinions clearly and forcefully. They said that they would go back to their group and discuss the situation and plan. They would let the organizers know of their decision.

The organizers were upset. If black students did not join with them, the validity of their position would be in question. After all, this was being done on behalf of the black cause for freedom and justice. I then made a statement myself. I explained that the time had come when a black man on campus had to speak for himself and decide for himself the proper course of action. Neither he nor any other white person could preempt that responsibility. Blacks were on campus, and they were there to stay. After that, I left the meeting, followed by the two black students.

The report was made to the black students, and their reaction was one of deep resentment. A general discussion ensued about what to do. After a while, I stated that whatever we did had to have two objectives in mind. First, that it did not directly or indirectly feed the Wallace assumption the "nigras" were among his good friends but not necessarily accountable for their emotional reaction to things they did not understand. Second, that whatever we did had to have impact on the campus that would give us the opportunity to do other things after Wallace had gone. I reminded them that we were not representing ourselves alone, but other black people of the community as well. They decided to form a committee to work out details, and then further meetings of the whole group would be held.

What emerged was beautiful in its simplicity and directness. We would print our own handbills that would be handed out to the crowd expected to attend the occasion. It would point out, among other things, that, if Alabama was symptomatic of the kind of administration we could expect from Mr. Wallace, not only blacks but everybody else would be in trouble. We would borrow a loudspeaker and play freedom songs interspersed with works of Countee Cullen, Frederick Douglass, and others. We would start this about an hour before Mr. Wallace was to enter the auditorium. The students would dress in dark clothes and sit in a body close to the front of the auditorium. If, during his speech, Mr. Wallace were to make statements deemed biased and prejudicial to the interests of black people, the students would rise quietly and leave the auditorium without comment. It sounded too simple to some, but I stated that at times the simple things were the most effective. We agreed to adopt the plan, and the group was soon engaged in feverish activity to get things moving. The white group was informed that we were going to do our own thing. They didn't like it, but there was nothing they could do about it.

The speech was to begin at eight o'clock. Our activities would begin at seven. Until then we would go about our usual business. The white student group went through its familiar patterns: petitions to the president asking him to call off the meeting, groups of chanting, placard-waving students in motley dress, parading through the campus. A rally was to be held before and after Mr. Wallace's speech in front of Whig-Clio. The administration officials were alerted to keep an eye on things to try to prevent incidents. The campus atmosphere was tense. Everyone knew that security measures would be tight.

The crowd began to gather outside of Dillon Gym at about a quarter of seven. The doors were supposed to open at seven o'clock.

For some unexplained reason, probably for added security precautions, the doors didn't open until seven-thirty. Our loudspeaker was positioned in the window of a dorm that fronted on the square just outside of Dillon Gym. We went into motion on the dot and had a captive audience. The students quietly distributed the handbills. The music was familiar and stirring. The poetry was read in clear, forceful, dramatic tones. The crowd was being entertained and informed of black opinion. Mr. Wallace entered the gym almost unnoticed. Coup number one!

Just before eight o'clock, the black students moved into the auditorium and took their seats. They were obvious and beautifully visible. Just before Mr. Wallace was introduced, someone from the white student group made an abortive attempt to leap on the platform and grab the microphone for an inflammatory speech to the audience. He was unceremoniously hustled off by the police. The crowd settled down. The introductions were made, and the speech began.

It was the same old speech. Complimentary remarks about Princeton and its place in the history of the country. Some quips about the students who had demonstrated earlier in the day and the incident preceding his speech. Standard provision intended to give him a feel for the audience. I had read the text of most of his speeches with great care. I had clued the students to about where he would launch into his subtleties and inferences about blacks. It usually occurred about two-thirds of the way through his speech. By that time, he had a feel for the audience and could get into the most controversial part of his talk. In other university appearances, this was the point at which student demonstrations or interruptions would occur. He would then treat this with a very cavalier attitude, and the audience would usually go along with him in the interest of fair play. It was a good ploy.

The audience was politely attentive. On cue, he launched into the part of his speech that attacked the black community. The students waited for him to get into the first paragraph of it, making sure that this was the tack he was going to take. Then, as if at a command, they rose and proceeded to file out of the auditorium. No gestures. No comments. A quiet, dignified, passionate response to bigotry. The eyes of the audience followed them. Mr. Wallace was taken aback. "Say something." "Give me a chance to explain." They moved toward the exit and vanished.

The next day the campus was buzzing. Indeed, the whole community was buzzing with the way in which the black students had handled themselves. My phone was ringing all day long. The black community: We were proud of the way the students handled the situation. The campus administration: The black students handled a difficult situation with dignity and directness. There was no doubt about their feelings. The white community: The black students gave an effective denial to the Wallace message! The white students: Where the hell did all those black guys come from? Are they Princeton? Black had become more significant than orange. I've never seen an orange man!

The black students were enthusiastic. For the first time, they had done something as a group. It was a real good "high." White students were stopping them to find out how they had come up with the idea. Then they asked, "What next?"

The time was ripe. They were ready. Now let's talk about organization. We had something to follow up on. Now, it's not uncommon for student organizations to spring up overnight on a college campus. As a matter of fact, it's expected and accepted as a fact of life on a college campus. The fact of a black college group on a white campus like Princeton had to have a presence. Just announcing the formation of a black student group on the Princeton campus was not going to do it. There had to be another ingredient.

I had brought a group of administrators from black colleges to Princeton for a conference on the problems their institutions encountered in attracting black and white students. The Princeton academic and general community had been impressed with their knowledge and their understanding of nationwide academic problems. It was the first of its kind at Princeton. What if we were to follow that with the first conference of black students from predominantly white institutions to discuss the future of black students involved in directing their own future? The subject was broached to the black student group. What? A conference of black students to be held at Princeton? Why not? Do you know of a better way to put your organization in motion and bring Princeton to the attention of other black students at the same time? Do you know of a better way to get rid of the appellation of Princeton as "the plantation" for black students? Okay. Let's get moving.

What the students did not know was that I had checked out the possibility of the university sponsoring a conference on a topic relevant to blacks. I had been told that the custom was to have a member of faculty, who was an expert on the subject, chair such a conference. Since there was no "expert" that they knew of, the University Conference Committee could not fund such an undertaking. I knew then that we would have to do whatever we wanted out of our own resources. It had already been decided that the announcement of the formation of a black student group on campus would be made two weeks before the conference. There were long debates over the name that the group should carry. We finally decided on "The Association of Black Collegians."

None of the students had participated in the development of a conference before, so I sat down with them and mapped out the structure that the conference should have. We set up committees that would carry out all of the work that had to be done. It was another kind of educational experience. I handled the task of trying to develop a funding base and informing the administration of what the group was going to do. It was important to follow protocol that governed the recognition of any student group on campus. There were certain benefits that accrued from official status as a Princeton organization. In the case of the Association of Black Collegians, it was utterly important that it have the backing and blessing of top administration if it were to have the status that I felt it needed in order to carry out the plans we had in mind.

I knew the task would be a difficult one. Princeton was an "open campus." That meant no person was to be denied access to membership in any club, organization, or facility because of race, color, or religion. Once a person was admitted to Princeton, he became a "son of Old Nassau" and that was that. I admired the principle, but knew that, in practice, there were nuances and subtleties that acted as inhibiting factors to black students.

There are two ways of "belonging" to any system. First, directly or indirectly, one can lay claim to having created or developed the various factors that make the system what it is. Second, one can become an attachment or appendage to an existing system by virtue of the tolerance of those who run the system. Any white student coming to Princeton could lay claim to any or all parts of it as an institution. He could take pride and satisfaction in the traditions and customs that defined the system and the institution. He could always lose himself in splendid anonymity and still lay claim, whenever he wanted to, to all that Princeton represented.

It was a white institution and system. No black could lay claim, with any validity, to anything that Princeton represented. In order for the black presence at Princeton to have an ongoing, defining role in future development, there had to be a way by which blacks could break their own ground, plant their own roots, and create their own systems that would become indigenous to Princeton in the hearts and minds of the campus and community.

This was the position from which I argued the case for an association of black students and for the black student conference to be sponsored by them in the name of Princeton.

I worked my way up the official ladder. First Brad, my immediate superior, then the dean, then the president. The sessions were tough. I asked no quarter, and they gave none. There were hard-hitting, critical, searching questions as to motivation and intent. There were hard-hitting, candid, logical responses. In the end, in spite of some personal hesitancy, there was agreement that, if I felt that this was good for Princeton, they would give it the support that was necessary. One of the things that I have always remembered about the men who held top positions at Princeton was the quality of fairness and openmindedness that they exhibited when it came to upholding the integrity of Princeton.

I had worked out a method of handling the costs of the conference that would make it unnecessary for the university to contribute anything but its facilities. A list of all possible expenses was carefully developed. I reasoned, if it became known that Princeton black students were sponsoring a conference dealing with the concerns of black people in the area of education, no institution would turn down the opportunity to send delegates from their own black student organizations. Therefore, we could charge them a delegate fee and ask them to pay for the students that they sent. When I put this to the dean, he thought I'd blown my stack. I said that if a letter went out over his signature to fellow deans at the institutions we had selected, I didn't see them not supporting him or Princeton. He said that it was worth a try.

His letter went to over fifty institutions selected by the students who knew where the black organizations were on white campuses. In addition, we invited several predominantly black institutions to send representatives under the same terms. The students had been on the job. Either by phone or in person, they had reached all of the black student organizations and informed them about the conference. They reported that the response was overwhelmingly enthusiastic. Most of them didn't believe that it would take place. Princeton? My God!

It would take about two weeks for the responses to the invitation to come back, if they were going to come at all. In the meantime, we kept on with the details, such as getting the conference space. (I had decided on the Woodrow Wilson School as the venue. It was the newest and most prestigious building on the campus. Besides, there was a gentle irony in holding a conference of black students in a place named after the man who had not proved to be a friend to blacks either at Princeton or in the nation. My own kind of private joke.) Arrangements for housing two hundred students for two days. Arrangements for feeding them. Selecting speakers. Providing entertainment. Setting up panel topics. Deciding on student panel chairmen.

After a week I could sense the tension mounting among the students. Maybe the invitations had gone astray. Maybe the schools were unwilling to pay the delegate fees. Maybe we should have started with a smaller effort and been assured of success. Maybe we should have copied what other black organizations had done and given a "Soul" party with a few people asked to speak but not make things too "heavy." Maybe, maybe, maybe.

To the students I maintained an outwardly calm and optimistic manner. Of course things would work. Patience. We were going to do this thing in the Princeton manner and give it the seriousness it deserved. Don't worry. Keep up with the arrangements. Things would have to be ship shape. We're going to do it up "brown." Away from the students, I had the same misgivings. My poor wife bore the brunt of my anxiety. She did for me what I was doing for the students. If she had any doubts, she kept them to herself.

Two of the student leaders of ABC, as we were to be known, were sitting in my office when the mail came with the first responses. I opened two of the letters and began to laugh. It had worked. "Yes! Of course they would be delighted to participate in the conference. Enclosed was a check for the delegates." I passed the letter over to Paul Williams and Deane Buchanan. Slow grins began to spread over their faces. Then they let go. We shook hands. Laughed. Shook hands again.

John stuck his head in the door. I told him about the responses. He grinned broadly, came into the room, and there was another round of hand shaking and back slapping. The students left to spread the news, and I hustled into Brad's office and told him that we were in. He gave his congratulations and said he would pass the word on to the dean. After that, there was a steady stream of acceptances, names of delegates, and money. Out of the fifty schools we had invited, forty-one had accepted and were sending delegates.

Two weeks before the conference, the *Daily Princetonian* carried the report of the formation of a new student group on campus, the Association of Black Collegians. It was a good, factual story. It gave the reasons for the formation of the group that had been prepared by the Black Collegians' public relations committee and listed the names of the officers. We all waited for the reaction.

The black community approved whole-heartedly of this development. The campus community was quiet. What was this? Why did they have to have their own association? The administration, by and large, made no comment. The students reported that they were stopped on campus, or visitors came to their rooms in order to talk about this new development. What about this conference? Could interested white students attend? Wasn't this reverse discrimination?

About the same time, I decided to act on an idea that had been forming in my mind for about two weeks. I was going to go "whole hog." "Come high or stay away," the crapshooters used to say. I was coming high! We needed someone to open the conference and welcome the delegates. We needed the mark of overt, total acceptance of what we were doing and what we represented to Princeton. Who could give us that? Who else? The president.

When I told the students of my decision, they were incredulous. They told me that I had been working too hard. If I thought "Bogey" would open that conference, I was really "way out." Sure, they would like to have him open the conference. No president of any college had ever attended, much less opened, any affair given by their black student organization.

I called the president's office and asked for an appointment. This was to be my second time in his office in the three years I had been there. After exchanging greetings, I wasted no time in getting to the topic. The students wanted him to open the conference and greet the delegates. I explained the importance of this to the students and went into the details of why this was important not only to them, but to the university. That he would be doing something that no other college or university president had done with respect to black student organizations.

Bob Goheen listened carefully with that characteristic little furrow between his eyes when he was concentrating on a problem of importance to the university. When I finished, he said that he was pleased that the students wanted him to be present on the occasion, but the time was so short that he wouldn't have time to prepare a speech. In addition, he already had a commitment for that afternoon and had planned to leave early in order to keep it.

I told him that I was aware of the shortness of time and that I didn't expect him to make a major speech. Five minutes of his time and presence was all that was necessary. He said that he would think it over and let me know his decision within a day. I thanked him and left the office with mixed feelings. I knew that he was busy and had a legitimate right to refuse the invitation. On the other hand, I felt that Bob was interested enough in anything that happened at Princeton, especially in the case of black students, to make an effort to be present. After all, it was through his initiative, out of a desire to make Princeton truly representative of a cross section of the nation, that the policy affecting black representation had come into being. I waited.

The next day I received a call from the president. Yes, he would open the conference on the understanding that he would not be giving a speech, but saying a few words of welcome to the assembled delegates. Fine! Thank you! I hopped around the office in glee. The gamble had paid off. I went straight to the dean's office and told him that the president had accepted the invitation to open the conference. Would he be available to open the second day of the conference and introduce the black speaker who had consented to give the major address? Yes! He'd be delighted!

I ran down to my office, taking two steps at a time. Thank you, God, for answering my prayer. Both of them at the same conference. Wow! When I passed the word on to the students, they couldn't believe it. Was I sure? When they found out I hadn't been joking, bedlam broke loose. But there was another effect that I had been looking for, and it came. They quieted down and began to talk about the fact that now they had to make the conference a success. They were really on the line. Suddenly, the tremendous importance of what they were about to do struck all of them. They grew from boys to men right before my eyes. I knew then that we were on target.

March 30, 1967 was a beautiful day in Princeton. The delegates had begun to arrive in droves. The students were taking care of room assignments in an efficient manner. The programs were on hand. Everything was going according to plan. Three students had been assigned to escort the president to the Woodrow Wilson School: Paul, the president of ABC, Deane, the vice president, and Badi Foster, the graduate student representative. The students were lined up just inside the glass doors and windows of Woodrow Wilson as the president of the university came up the steps. I was standing to one side and could see his expression as he came through the door. It was one of surprise and pleasure. He had never seen all of the black students of the university together before.

I introduced each student to him by name, and he shook hands with each one of them. They were a fine-looking group of students. They had a dignity all their own, befitting the situation. We moved into the auditorium and again, Bob was struck with surprise and pleasure. Looking up, he was gazing into the eyes and faces of two hundred black college and university students representing the cream of the institutions of the eastern seaboard. There were several white administrators in the audience. They were like marshmallows in a chocolate sea.

I introduced Robert Goheen, the president of Princeton, and there was a murmur of approval throughout the audience. They greeted him with polite applause. Seated to one side, I could see the two or three small cards that held the notes Bob would be using. Okay. I had five minutes. I was looking out at the audience when I suddenly became aware that something had happened. The script was off key. I glanced at the cards in Bob's hand and realized that he wasn't referring to them at all. I looked at his face and realized that this was no perfunctory greeting of welcome to Princeton. Bob had taken off!

For the next thirty minutes, he held the audience in rapt attention as he spelled out his own conviction about the necessity of equality of opportunity at all levels of society and especially in the sphere of education. He acknowledged the inequities of the past but urged the students to look forward to the future, to make the most of their opportunity in gaining an education that would help them to be in the vanguard of new achievements and progress for their people and for the United States as a whole.

Every eye was glued on him. They were taking in every word. When he finished, there was an outpouring of applause before he could take his seat. In one spontaneous motion, the audience rose to its feet and rocked Woodrow Wilson auditorium with a tribute that I have seldom seen accorded a white man by a black student group. It was from the heart, and it spoke of appreciation for not the mere word, but the feelings from the heart and soul of a man. Bob rose and waved his hand at the group, a quivering smile on his lips. He was moved.

The conference was off to a great start. The black students of Princeton watched him with pride as Bob moved out of the auditorium. He was their president! They were Princeton!

CHAPTER 5

I'VE NEVER SEEN AN ORANGE MAN

Wisdom is not necessarily a concomitant of old age. I didn't coin that statement, but I'll buy into it. The United States, almost two hundred years old, still values and rates people according to color instead of their status as human beings. The myth of racial superiority based on color is still being espoused by certain scientists and denounced by other human beings. Princeton is older than the United States, and, up to the year 1963, there was no evidence that they were any wiser about the abilities and capabilities of people of a different color to handle its academic chores as students or run its establishment as administrators. To give it due credit though, I must say that, in seven or eight years, its wisdom about people has almost approximated its years in existence. Whether the two will ever be balanced off is for the future to tell. I don't have any crystal ball.

By the time the 1967-1968 academic year rolled around, the black student group, or ABC as it was now known by everyone, was firmly entrenched in the Princeton scene. The Family Sponsor Program was in full swing. It was almost as though it had always been there. The family sponsors were to begin a series of meetings with the dean of the college that was to be a real milestone in black community-Princeton University relations. For the first time, a group of black people could register their concern about the conduct of affairs pertinent to and affecting the black student body. I must pay tribute to Ed Sullivan, who had assumed the deanship in 1966. It was largely through his open-mindedness and sensitivity of spirit to the plight of deprived minorities that much of the progress of the next few years was to take place. I could usually count on Ed Sullivan and Bob Goheen to take the gamble if it meant improvement for the university, especially in the area of race relations.

The success of the conference had gone a long way to establish the reputation of ABC as a positive force on the campus. The academic standing of the students was in line with all other groups on campus. Especially gratifying was the academic performance of the two students that had been asked to leave the university for a year pending their performance in other institutions. They had both returned with upper-level marks from their institutions and had continued good academic performance at Princeton.

Shortly after the turn of the new year, a group of Jewish students came to my office to ask if I would assist them in the formation of a Jewish student association. It seemed that, since the emergence of the black students as a group, other minorities on the Princeton campus saw no reason not to become visible in their own right.

I was terribly intrigued by this state of affairs. For years, whenever a member of another minority group in the United States had proclaimed sympathy and oneness with the black minority, I had said it was not the same thing. Irish, Jewish, Italian, Greek, or whatever, he had the advantage of what I termed "protective coloration." As long as he was white or looked like he was white, he had an advantage no black person could claim. This is what had given rise to the light-complexioned black's tendency to "pass." There was "passing" of another kind evinced by people of other ethnic groups who felt that this was necessary in order to deal with the "WASP" control of basic opportunities.

I can always remember the concern that one of my colleagues from a minority group expressed at the tactics I was beginning to develop in my first few years at Princeton. He constantly reminded me of where I was and would caution me against being too obvious about what I was as a black. I used to tell him, and anybody else that was interested, that I saw no reason to make believe I was something other than a black man. Who would believe me anyway? I could speak a foreign language, wear different clothes, or marry someone from a different culture. If I looked black, in the United States, I was black. And that was that. Very few whites will ever understand the mystique that surrounded a man like Congressman Adam Clayton Powell, Jr., who looked white, but talked and acted black.

I did ask the Jewish students who came to see me why they had not contacted someone of their own faith, but I really didn't make an issue of it. They had come, as Princeton students, to seek my assistance, and I was glad to help them in whatever they had decided was right to do and in the interests of a better Princeton. In our discussion of goals and purposes, I discovered they were concerned about the recent exacerbation of relations between blacks and Jews in urban centers of the United States, especially the East Coast cities like New York and Philadelphia. They wanted to bring together Jewish students from other eastern universities for discussion of problems and what they could do about lessening tension and creating better understanding on their campuses and in the cities.

I suggested Mr. James Farmer, former director of CORE, as a speaker. He agreed to come. The conference was planned as a two-day affair, beginning on Friday with a Sabbath service. I was invited to the service and worshipped and fellowshipped with the students and their guests as the only black man in the congregation. On the way home that evening, I heard news of the assassination of Dr. Martin Luther King, Jr. My wife and I had been invited to a party that evening. We decided to go. There were about a dozen other people there. All of us were shaken by the news and sat in quiet discussion about what this would portend for the future of the country.

The next morning, I met with the Jewish students to discuss the effect of this tragedy on their program. They decided to forego the planned events and ask Mr. Farmer to speak to a larger assemblage, including black and white students from the university and the community. When Jim Farmer arrived, he consented to do this. His reflections on the life and times of Dr. King and the need to carry out the work he had started fitted in perfectly with the theme of the conference. Jim is one of the gifted orators of the country, and when he finished speaking, the congregation linked hands and sang "We Shall Overcome" with a spirit of dedication and feeling that I think few of them had ever experienced before.

On Monday I met with the leaders of ABC. The group had met all day on Sunday formulating plans for a memorial tribute to Dr. King. On the day of the funeral service they wanted to hold seminars all over the campus, led by black students, but open to the entire academic community. They felt that this was a propitious moment for a sober discussion of race relations, justice, and equality for all men. They asked me if I would contact the president for permission to hold this kind of memorial instead of having classes. I agreed to carry out their wishes.

Bob was very moved by the tragedy of Dr. King's death but had his own ideas about the kind of memorial that was fitting to his life and works. Dr. King had spoken at the chapel on a couple of occasions and had made a deep impression on Bob and all who had heard him. Bob felt that the best way for black and white students to honor Dr. King was to carry on with the academic work of the university and thereby prepare themselves for the opportunities that Dr. King had advocated. A memorial service had already been planned which the whole university and community could attend. He knew that I had been asked to deliver the eulogy and that black students would have a prominent part in the service. He felt this was enough.

I conveyed his decision to ABC. The students were incensed at what they considered a disregard for their feelings in this matter. I had warned Bob that the reaction to his decision might evoke a strong response from the ABC, but he felt that reason would prevail. I didn't know what was going to happen. It's a good thing that I didn't. I might have felt constrained to interfere with the students' proposed action and that would have been a serious mistake.

The next morning, I was called to the dean's office for an urgent meeting. I was told about the action that had been taken by ABC. The group had marched, in a body, to the president's home at about 11 p.m. the previous evening and had asked him to reconsider his decision. They told him that, as black people, they had deep feelings about what had occurred that he didn't seem to understand. They stated that they were coming to him in recognition and respect for him and his office before they took any other action. If he did not reconsider and close down classes for the day as they had requested, they would be forced to take other means to close down the campus.

Bob had listened carefully to the students' spokesman and had sensed that they indeed felt that they were being driven to a course of action that would go beyond the conventional bounds. Bob had always reacted negatively to threats, either direct or indirect. But this was not an ordinary situation, and his reaction was tempered accordingly. He promised that they would have his decision the next morning.

All of the top administration was very upset by the students' action. Did I know what they were going to do? No, I did not. Was I surprised at their action? No, I was not, and I had warned the president that his decision would not be taken lightly. In the light of actions taken by students on other campuses, I thought they had behaved with considerable restraint. They could have wrecked the campus first and talked afterwards. Instead, they had acted like responsible members of the community. Did I have any clues as to what they might do if the president remained firm on his original decision? No, I didn't have the faintest idea. Would I persuade them to accept the president's decision? No, I would not.

About an hour later, I received a call from the president's office and went over to see him. Bob let me know that he considered the students' action as a severe breach of conduct and propriety. Under other circumstances, he would have felt forced to take swift disciplinary action. He had carefully considered the situation, however, and had decided to permit the university to be closed for regular academic study and all the ABC seminars to be carried on instead. He insisted that there be no undue coercion on the part of the ABC to force people to come to the seminars. It must be on a voluntary basis.

I agreed to pass his decision on to the students. I suggested that it would be politic if he sent his own statement to the *Daily Princetonian* about the cessation of classes. That would obviate any rumors or idle speculation about who had brought pressure on whom. He agreed.

On the day of the funeral, I was sent as a representative from Princeton to the services in Atlanta. The seminars on the Princeton campus were held in a commendable fashion. All of the seminars were full. Not every student or faculty member attended, but there was genuine agreement from those who did that it was a worthwhile experience.

Later that week, the ABC announced that they would hold a silent vigil in Palmer Square in honor of Dr. King. It would last for one hour between 11:00 a.m. and 12:00 noon. At about 11:30 a.m. on the day of the vigil, I left my office and walked over to the square. There must have been about two hundred people standing there. As I got closer, I could see that the inner circle was all black. Students from the university and the town were gripping hands across their bodies. Tight lipped. Grim faced. Silent. Some with heads bowed. Some looking straight ahead with motionless eyes. Outside of the circle stood silent white students and adults. The only movement was the shuffling of feet as persons moved in or out of the crowd. I looked around from the outside and then moved closer to the black ring. It was impressive. A show of solidarity in a visible way that Princeton had never seen before. Black people standing together, honoring a black leader.

I became conscious of a young white teenager standing close to me and close to the ring. I looked at her and saw tears streaming down her cheeks, her shoulders shaking with barely controlled sobbing. She raised her head and spoke out to no one in particular. "Why can't I join the circle and hold hands?" she exclaimed. "I loved Dr. King. He spoke for me, too." By God, she was right.

A few paraphrased words ran through my head. What had King said that day, standing in front of the Lincoln Memorial in Washington, D.C.? Wasn't it something about a day that would see all men, regardless of color, joining hands in brotherhood to fight for justice, equality, and freedom? Black brotherhood and unity. YES. But not until there was a joining with other kinds of brotherhood and unity would all be free. I reached out and grabbed the hand of the girl, moved between two black students and grasped the hand of the one on my right. I looked over at the other student. His eyes were resentful, his body tensed. We looked at each other for what seemed like a long second. Then he reached for the outstretched hand of the white girl and resumed his stance. Jesus! There's still a lot to overcome!

After the memorial week, things returned to normal; that is, students went back to classes, professors taught, administrators administered various and sundry things. But the new, vibrant, black presence on the campus had made its mark. Stories were written by and about the plight of the black student on the Princeton campus. Blacks held their heads high as they walked across the campus or through the streets of the town. It looked good and felt good.

Personally, I had been giving a great deal of thought to my continued stay at Princeton. In the four years that I had been there, I had worked for Princeton and for black students. On both ends, I felt that I had done all that I had been expected to do and maybe a little more. I was getting restless. There were other jobs to do and other ways that I could profitably spend my time. I had already been contacted by places that offered some new opportunities back in New York. I was ready to leave. Princeton was a closed corporation as far as I was concerned. Once put, stay put, was not my idea of progress. Besides, I had often spoken to the students about the necessity for being prepared in order to take advantage of legitimate opportunities that occurred, be it where you were or someplace else. I couldn't talk about it and not do it!

So one morning in late April, I went to Brad's office to tell him of my decision to leave. Brad got about as upset as I had ever seen him. He said that he thought I was being premature. There were still things to be done. Was I unhappy? Had anything happened that he had been unaware of? I leveled with him. After I had finished, he said that he would like a chance to talk with the dean. I said okay.

A few days later, I was called to the dean's office. Ed said that Brad had told him I was going to leave. Why? I told him the same thing that I had told Brad. Ed said that leaving now would leave a real gap in the work I was doing. I reminded him of the fact that there was now another black man in the bureau office. He could carry on. I had shared with him just about all that I had been doing. Ed asked me to defer any final decision until he had talked with the president. Again I agreed.

By this time I was getting interested in what might come up. I knew what I wanted in the way of a position. If I were going to continue there, I wanted into the power sector of the university, where policy was decided. A position from which I would be able to help set policy before it was cut and dried for others to follow. I had said little about this because, from where I sat, that was too far out for Princeton to consider.

Later that week I was sitting in the president's office. Ed had told him I was ready to leave, and he wanted to hear from me what the reasons were. I told him. Bob listened carefully, as was his wont, and then asked me what it would take to get me to stay. Wow! Okay, he had asked for it. So I let go. After about ten minutes of talking on my part, Bob said he would like time to think some things over. He would be in touch with me in a short while. In the meantime, would I agree not to make any definitive moves? I concurred.

True to his word, I was called into his office a few days later. He had talked with Ed, Brad, and a few other people. He thought he had a position that would interest me. Would I consider the position of Assistant Dean of the College as being in the realm of what I wanted? I sat still for a while, thoughts racing around in my head. Was he serious? Damn! I looked at Bob. He was serious. That sounded fine I said, but I'd like to have time to think it over.

Bob was quick to pick this up. Was there anything else? After all, if I accepted, I would become the first black dean in Princeton's history. Yes, I was aware of that, but besides that, what would it mean? He looked somewhat puzzled. I didn't leave him that way for long.

The position was great, but in order to mean something to black and white people outside and inside the university, I had to represent, not just a position, but clout. An equal access to policy and power. Like what? Well, I had observed that the university had no machinery set up to deal with the human relations aspect of higher education. I accepted the fact that a university was a community of scholars, but scholars were also people. Bob thought about this for a while. Then he said that he would call me in a few days for further talks on the matter.

I walked up the stairs to my office, lit a cigarette, and called my favorite confidante, John, into the office. I told him what I had been offered. His face lit up with pleasure. "Man, it's about time those people woke up to the fact that you're needed here." I rather expected John to be pleased, but what about the others? Brad already knew, and when I talked to him about it, said that he was of the opinion that I should take the job; I had earned it. Ed said that he would be pleased to have me as one of his assistants. I knew that he had to concur in the decision because I would be working much more closely with him and the policy of the dean's office. He laughed as he remarked that he had never dreamed of becoming a dean of Princeton because he thought he came from the wrong side of the tracks. Now I was his assistant. By God! Princeton would never be the same with an Irishman and a black working together. I joined in his amusement.

Two days later, I was in Bob's office again. He had decided to offer me the chairmanship of the president's newly created university Human Relations Committee. In that role, I would be entitled to sit on the university Administrative Policy Committee. I knew what that meant. I didn't waste any more time. I accepted both positions.

Neither the black students, my wife, my family, nor my friends could deal with the news when I told them. Unbelievable. Fantastic. Are you sure? I was sure. It was agreed that the official announcement would be held off until just before graduation. That was all right with me. It would give me a chance to get myself together and my thoughts in order about this new responsibility and how it could be used.

I was still reveling in the idea of the new position when something else occurred to me. The 1968 commencement exercises would see the largest number of black students receiving a Princeton diploma in its history. Eight. All eight of the ones who had come in four years before. They had been a cadre that had worked with me during those years. Two of them had been outstanding in their leadership with both black and white students. Something should be done to recognize the time and effort they had put into making Princeton a better place for black and white students alike. I fanned through past commencement and awards exercises and realized that no black person as a student had ever been awarded an honor for service to Princeton.

If black students had contributed to the advancement and development of Princeton through service to students and the community, why shouldn't they be recognized for their effort? If, as we had maintained, black manhood and peoplehood, with its own virtues and qualities, had been proven to be a vital ingredient in the recent history of Princeton, why not recognize it?

The questions were cogent. The next step was implementation. I examined all of the citations and decided that the one that would fit my purpose was a service award given in the name of a former president of Princeton. I took that as a model and changed the text to fit the service that had been done by black students. Next step: show it to Brad and John, both Princeton alumni, and get their reactions. Heads, I won. Then up to Ed. Heads, I won again. Two out of three. Will you go for three out of three? I will. On to Bob. Heads, I won again.

Bob posed the $64,000 question. Who do we name it after? I had given further thought to the name. I had listed the names of four black leaders that I thought would be appropriate for the award. Two were living, two were dead. Knowing Princeton and the thinking patterns of people who would have to make the decision, I kind of rigged the decision. We decided to call it the Frederick Douglass Award. The other names were either too current or too controversial. But, as I suspected, whites, even the very intelligent one, do not make the same associations that blacks do with their heroes and leaders. Douglass, along with Du Bois, was being quoted all over the place by black militants. As a matter of fact, his detailed designs were among the models used by Stokely Carmichael, Rap Brown, and a host of other "militants" given high esteem by the black population. In addition, Douglass had all of the respectability accorded by all kinds of liberals for his acute, academic analysis of the status of black people.

Through friends of mine, I had located the sculptress, Inge Hardison, who had produced the busts of well-known black leaders that were dispensed through a liquor company all over the United States. I called Inge, went up to her apartment, and bought two busts of Frederick Douglass to be awarded to the black student recipients. The dean asked me if I wanted to make the awards at the ceremony. I told him that he should make them. He had been very close to this group of students, had cooperated almost beyond the call of duty. The award should be seen as one coming from the recognized Princeton hierarchy and the university itself.

The day of the ceremony came. I was waiting impatiently for the award ceremony itself to get underway. Then came the moment: An award for the student who had exhibited, through his service, the highest principles of Princeton and the dedication to black ideals of progress and advancement. There were dual winners of the award. I stood behind the dean as Paul Williams and Deane Buchanan came down from the student ranks and walked forward to receive the award. The students, who had listened carefully to the text of the citation and who understood its significance, rose as one body, black and white, in rousing ovation. People who did not know the significance of what was happening were caught up in the enthusiasm that engulfed the students. Paul and Deane walked confidently forward to the dean, received their awards, shook hands, and returned to their places amid the now deafening roar of applause and cries of "Right On!" I stood there, choking back tears and watching this Princeton crowd cheering the accomplishments of black students.

Later in the day, as I was leaving the office in the company of my wife, I crossed paths with the president. "Good evening, Dean Fields," he said, with a smile on his face. I grinned and said, "Good evening, Mr. President."

CHAPTER 6

ICING ON THE CAKE

To the world of Princeton and to the outside community, I was what could be described as "a successful black." I held a position no one like me had held before. I was on more committees than I knew what to do with. I was in demand as a lecturer, consultant, and recipient of honors. I guess if I hadn't been through this before, I would have taken it much more to heart than I did. But I had had prior experience. As a high school and college athlete, I was among the best in my specialty. I'd had the thundering cheers of thousands of people ringing in my ears after I'd won an event. In my brief fling at concert work, I had bowed to the applause of all kinds of audiences. Others, more famous than I in their own right, have had the same experience. I had also had the experience of walking into the same athletic arena or concert hall as a guest or patron and not being noticed by anybody. Being successful, as modern society understands it and applauds it, can be an enervating and static experience.

Before taking the new titles and positions, I had called in the leadership of the Black Collegians and told them what I thought was going to happen. I would not be as close to them physically as I had been in the past. Once I took a position in the "system," I would be open to all kinds of innuendos and inferences as to what I represented and how much in tune I still was with the things that had been accomplished. In our terms that meant "how black" you still were. Those two words have infinite meaning within the current black society. They can do you in or do you up. If the leadership of ABC had not understood its role in that whole business, I would have had serious reservations about taking the position. I was in a new role; they would have to assume some share in that new role as well. They did.

I was fraught. For one thing, once you have been let "inside," no matter what you have done before that, you're kind of expected to be the same as all the other insiders. That's a tricky position to be in whether you're black or white! If you hang too much, too obviously, to the outside, you run the risk of being labeled an "eccentric." That means that they'll tolerate almost anything you will do short of a felony and write it off as having no effect on what they or anyone else wants to do. There were a number of people like that at Princeton.

On the other hand, if you bought into everything, they could figure that all the things you had done before was to reach for a position from which you could be comfortable. In academic terms they call that tenure. In many cases, when you get tenure, you can do the same things that you became famous or successful for without very many people questioning the relevancy of what you're doing.

I played it loose right from the jump; there was no point in tightening up now. This is when I began to understand that the Black Administrator had to be a Black Educational Statesman. He had a constituency to represent, but there were other constituencies that he had to be cognizant of. The "Black Cause" was a solid, dominant wedge to open the doors, but you could be damn sure that once the door was open, others were sitting there, suffering under the same things, who would want and even demand the same things that blacks had achieved. I can remember people telling me that if they did it for blacks, they would have to do it for everybody. It was a curious admission that they had done it for precious few. I was right. It wasn't long before I was approached by Puerto Ricans, Chinese, Indians, and other kinds of groups that believed they had a special right to be included in organizations or movements that would give them a purchase at Princeton.

From 1968 to the beginning of 1971, things moved with incredible rapidity. The first thing that I took on full blast was the admissions system. I argued if Princeton wanted to become a national university, it had to have national representation of the population. That meant that eleven percent of the Princeton student body had to be black. This was accepted in principle, but they maintained that, with their best efforts, they didn't think they would be able to find that kind of representation. I maintained that their criteria for achievement was not broad enough to include the kinds of things that black kids really could present as credentials other than academic marks.

After several crucial meetings, it was decided to include "work experience," that is, real work experience of the sort necessary for survival, in addition to the kind that most of the affluent participated in for fun and experience. By that time, I had begun to understand that "affluent" could mean "smart and white" no matter what the economic condition, or just white, or just affluent in the real sense. By that time also, I had met a number of Princeton alumni who had told me that they came from poor and humble circumstances to the university and were cognizant of all the disadvantages that they felt accrued to them from that condition.

With the broadening of the criteria for admission, I knew that the numbers situation would take care of itself. The next thing I understood and conveyed to top administration was that the phenomenal success we had experienced with black students over the years from 1964-1968 could not be expected to continue. The ninety-eight percent retention and progress rates were unreal. Eventually, the black students at the university would exhibit all the characteristics of the normal student population. When that began to occur, they should be ready to deal with it the way they would any normal student condition. Black students were no angels. They took drugs, they stole, they could cheat on exams, they could do all the things that a normal student population was subject to. When they would begin to feel comfortable enough and behave as Princeton students, they were not to be treated as people outside the pale. It was a good thing that I had stated this because the first time that a black student was found definitely in the wrong, they were ready to throw the book at him. When I reminded them that the black student's offense was no more heinous than that of the relative of a very prominent public official, they began to understand and deal with what I had meant.

By 1969-1970, a lot of things had begun to boil. Princeton was probably the only campus in the Ivy League and other predominantly white institutions that had not experienced a black student eruption. I knew we were due. The question was around what issue. By that time, we had black representation on a number of committees dealing with student concerns on the campus and in the community. The blow point would have to be something else.

The investment policy of the university in places like South Africa had been a sore point with black students for a long time. They had requested a meeting with the Board of Trustees and had had a chance to present their grievance. The board had listened and had been impressed with the sincerity and the presentation of the students but had decided that the evidence did not warrant their pulling out of their South African investment policy. Having had a little more experience with things where investment money or policy was involved, I had my own ideas as to how effective they would be with a group of pragmatic business men. But the main thing was that they had had an opportunity to present their case as Princetonians. It added to their status that people took kindly to their effort.

Midway through the 1969-1970 academic year, the coordinator of ABC, Rod Hamilton, came into the office for one of his informal chats. He intimated that the tenor of the students was to take more definitive action about Princeton's investment policy. I asked what they had in mind. Rod was very cagey and wouldn't commit himself but wanted to know what my position would be if they took an "extreme action." I said to him what I had said to his predecessors, "What are you going to do tomorrow?" Rod took more of a socialistic stance than a democratic one. "If this is what the masses feel is good and necessary, this is where I am and this is what I do." My response to that was that it had to come off clean, and the group had to be able to follow up what it would do with some advantage. We left it at that.

About a week later, I was scheduled to give a lecture to a group of black students at the Princeton Theological Seminary. When I entered the class, the professor was surprised and said that he thought that I would be over at the university. I asked why. He said that black students had taken over a building on the campus. I asked him if he still wanted me to go through with the lecture. He said that, in view of the circumstances, he would understand if I wanted to get back to my office.

I went over to my office. I knew what was going to happen. The Dean of Students would call me. The Dean of the College would call me. They would both want to know if I knew what was going on. I didn't. I knew what my channels of communication were like. Joe Moore, a native of Princeton, had taken the job of Assistant

Dean of Students. He was black. Joe had been in close touch with the students. If anyone knew what was going on at that point, it was Joe. I sat and waited for a report. The deans wanted to know if I would go down to the occupied building and talk to the students. I said that I didn't think so. They said that the president had ordered all responsible administrators to go there and try to get the kids out of the building. I said that I was not responsible for their being there and therefore saw no reason to go down there. I would wait in my office. If the students knew where I was, I felt sure that someone would contact me.

Joe checked in and told me what had happened. He had talked to Rod and some of the other students. He said that they had things under control and would call me later. I asked him what building they had taken over. He said it was the building where the Controller's office was located. That was the money building. Good show.

About an hour later, the phone rang. "Hey Doc, you know where we are?" the voice said. I recognized Rod's voice and said, "Yes, I know where you are. How are things going?" He said that they had things under control. Was I going to come down? No. What was the point? He didn't expect me to try to talk them out of there, did he? No. Well, I would wait until they got out, and then we could talk. Yep. About four or five o'clock. Crazy. If I didn't see them that day, I would see them tomorrow. Just make sure that everything was left in good order. Sure, they'd see to that.

Shortly thereafter, the public relations officer came to see me and ask what I thought of the situation. I told him that the students felt they had a legitimate case and that they felt that the university authorities had not taken them seriously. How soon would they be out? Well, if things went as I felt they would, they ought to be out at about five p.m. Could he tell that to the president? Sure. I sat in the office all day taking care of the business of the university. Joe came by to report that the white student leftist group had tried to get into the building and had been turned down by the ABC. Okay. They had remembered. If it's your cause, you fight for it yourself. Once you've established the groundwork, then you can accept the help of others and tell them how it should be delivered.

The next day, Rod, Len, Tshombe, and one or two more were in my office. What did I think would happen to them? I really didn't know. What they had to do now was go back to their academic work and make sure that was covered. Don't give out any more statements than were absolutely necessary and make sure that all statements were checked for accuracy and authenticity. Give me time to check out the scene and the attitudes.

For the next few days, I was involved in discussions with most of the top-level people in administration. They were of the opinion that something would have to be done that would serve as a lesson to the rest of the student body. I inquired as to what they had in mind. Well, suspension, if not expulsion, from the university. On what grounds? Violations of university rules and regulations. Where were these rules? I had not been able to find them. There was no regulation of the university that really covered what the students had done. They had occupied a building for a limited period of time. They had left the building in better order than they had found it. University property, per se, was intact. They had eaten some food. What were they going to be charged with? At most, they had stopped people from working for the day. Had they really disrupted university operations or interfered with university business to any great extent? I realized that they had wounded some university feelings, but was that cause to take the action they were considering?

In fact, there was no university regulation covering what the students had done, because it had never been done before. There was a general regulation against vandalism or destruction of university property, but nothing like that had taken place. I knew that something would have to be done, and in a few days I had come up with what I thought was a satisfactory solution. Confine the students to the campus. Warn them that any action like the one they had taken would, in the future, be grounds for suspension or expulsion from the university. Put the whole campus on record in that respect. Let the students appear before the university disciplinary committee. Examine the reasons for their actions and then let justice take its course. The punishment would have to fit the crime, so to speak.

My recommendation was not totally palatable to the administration, but they bought it. New rules were laid down covering the action and anything similar to it, and, for the first time, the university was covered. But the important thing was that the regulations affected all students, not just the black population.

The students had another opportunity to make their case against investment in South Africa. I was told how ably they had presented their case and how impressed members of the board were with their speech, demeanor, and logic. I responded with surprise that they should have thought anything different would occur. Weren't these Princeton students? What did they expect to happen? I must admit that I was a little smug about it, but then I had reason to be and so did they.

From the vantage point of membership in the administrative policy-making body, I had the opportunity to gain an overall picture of the university administration that you don't get from the lower echelons. Instead of operating through intermediaries, I could deal directly with the various shades of opinion, which could or would affect decisions or policies. In many instances it was the explanation or clarification that I could bring to discussions about the present and future condition of black and other minority students that would spell the difference between acceptance or rejection of proposals aimed at their welfare.

It was during this period that three other developments took place that were to be of material benefit to minority students and to Princeton as a whole. The first of these was the self-help orientation program for new black and other minority students. The use of the terms "black" and "minority" are used deliberately to identify what was beginning to be of real importance to Princeton's new student trend. In the recruiting that was done by black students, they hit schools with large black and other minority groups. We had agreed that we would recruit any likely minority student, regardless of ethnic factors that dictated color differences. As a result, we were getting small groups of Puerto Ricans, Mexican Americans, Indians, and Chinese as potential students. As each of these groups began to emerge, they began to react in their own way to the Princeton scene. If we weren't careful, the black student body, which was solidly entrenched as a force on campus, could draw the ire and resentment from other minority students that blacks had evidenced toward the white-student domination. Internecine conflict was bad news in my book.

By now, we had a black Assistant Dean of Students, Joe Moore, a native of Princeton, and Roberto Barragan, a young Cuban who had spent much of his life in the United States. Both of them had background and experience in social work and were invaluable in dealing with the varied aspects of student opinion and reaction. Together we planned the development of a student orientation program that would be manned by students and into which members of faculty and administration could be drawn as needed.

The rationale for this program was simple. Generally speaking, black and other minority students were alien to the life and traditions of a place like Princeton. Our task was to familiarize them, as rapidly as possible, with the methods, procedures, characteristics, and social conditions that prevailed so as to give them an opportunity to start out on an equal basis with students for whom the environs were less strange. The Family Sponsor idea had been brought inside. It was particularly focused on the students who were interested in or were committed to the study of science or engineering. Based on past experience, I knew that this was a trouble area for all students who were not familiar with the Princeton scheme. For black and other minority students, it could be twice as difficult if no help were offered.

Intelligence or aptitude per se was of little help to the student. I've seen students with above-average IQs flunk out of the School of Engineering. There was very little in the way of applied engineering subject matter. It was mostly a highly theoretical and sophisticated approach to the intricacies of engineering. It was important that the black and other minority students who entered these programs be as ready as we could make them for what they would experience.

The special-assistance programs that had been spawned by federal legislation had met with varying degrees of success on most college campuses. The administration was not enthusiastic about bringing anything like that to the campus and neither was I. I had quite a lot of experience with the programs and some of the students who had participated in them. I was aware of the pitfalls that had beset many an earnest effort. On the other hand, I was aware that Princeton had its own kind of student assistance programs that had operated informally for years. The orientation program was pitched to this level with more intensity and more organization for specific clientele. After orientation, the students were followed in a variety of ways, and help, when it was needed, was readily available. Faculty was alerted to the program effort and was enlisted in delivering to us their comments and cautions about students who were in danger of failing, as early as the first marking period. Roberto and Joe were responsible for the student tutors, each of whom was assigned a small group of freshmen. When by mid-year only four out of twelve black and other minority students were in serious academic distress, we had begun to prove our point. The cutting edge was not intelligence but familiarization with process and conditions.

The second development was more serious and was a direct outcome of the outmoded traditions and customs of the university. Although almost every university will lay claim to being a community of scholars, not many will say anything about the fact that scholars are people, too. The peoplehood of academia is taken for granted. It was this attitude of neglect for the person that gave rise to, among other things, the student rebellions of the sixties. It is necessary for a university to have rules and regulations that give order to its business just like any other branch or segment of society. But like any other branch of society, rules and regulations can become more important than the people to whom they apply. You can be bounced out of an institution very fast for violating the "honor code" but be given a mild reprimand for violating the personhood of an individual by calling him an offensive name.

Princeton, like many other residential institutions, is a community within a community. Like any community, as it grew, it developed residential patterns. The patterns resembled small neighborhood enclaves linked to a social center that was a club. Members of the club were selected by a set of rules and regulations set forth by the club denoting a group. Residential groupings were subject to less formal, but no less formidable rules and regulations. I had occasion more than once to talk to a student who had bid into a residence according to university rules only to be told by the occupants that he was not wanted for one reason or another.

In my first two years at the university, black students who were not athletes complained about suspected discrimination in the residence grouping. All athletes, black or white, were put in with teammates. I took this up with the administration and was told that it was probably accidental because they did not know the racial designation of the person assigned to a room. I suggested that, since there was such a small number of black students, they be deliberately assigned to multi-racial situations. There was a good bit of concern over this suggestion since about one-half of the student body was drawn from the South. I then suggested not only a mixed racial situation, but a mixed regional grouping as well. I maintained that it was better to err on the side of Princeton as an open campus than it was to be accused indirectly of discriminatory practices in housing.

With great misgivings on the part of the head of the room assignment service, my suggestions were adopted. This applied only to entering freshmen. It stayed in effect until there was a large enough group of black students on the campus to change the design. In the four years that it obtained, only one incident occurred that could broadly be termed an inter-racial clash. I handled that situation, and it was satisfactorily resolved on both sides.

By the academic year 1968-69, a major social change had taken place. Martin Luther King, Jr. had been assassinated, and passive resistance was on its way out. Stokely Carmichael, Rap Brown, James Baldwin, Leroi Jones (Imamu Baraka), et al., were in the ascendancy. Black is beautiful! Proud to be black! Black doesn't back down to anyone! The slogans of the day were replete with the new black consciousness. The students we were getting were more belligerent, more vocal right from the beginning about what they expected and what they wanted. By now we had a sizable black student community, and they wanted to be together.

I went to the dean and suggested that we change what had been the residential pattern for black students. It was simpler this time. I could take this up directly since I was part of the "system." He agreed black students could live together right from the beginning if they chose to do so. Okay. I knew that this would cause problems, but that's the way it is. Right! Another enclave was put into the neighborhood pattern.

By and large the black students had rejected the eating club system at the university. In the first place, they did not have to depend on it for social contacts. They had the black community. In the second place, the clubs did not represent to them their kind of "fun." Black jokes were not white jokes. Black soul music was not white country folk music. Black entertainment was not white entertainment. Those who did accept bids to join the clubs did so by design. Get in and then bring your friends. I can remember the consternation that greeted the rejection by black students of some of the more popular clubs on campus. We opened up and asked them to come in join us and they refused. How come? It was an age-old story: join us when we need you, not when you want to. It began to be a negative mark against any club if it didn't have at least one black student as a member. How else can you show your liberalness?

In the dormitories, the residential block that the black students had chosen was not far from that of some members of the football team. Little by little, stories began to find their way to me of some of the incidents that were beginning to take place. Most of them were trivial, and the students paid no attention to them. There were incidents involving students who had imbibed too much of one kind of strong liquid or another, meeting black students with their girlfriends and making insulting remarks, and black students being chased into their residences in the late hours of the night.

I called in the black student leaders and reminded them that they had to exercise due restraint, but that under no circumstances were they to let themselves be physically assaulted. It was not long before some of the white students, emboldened by what they felt was timidity on the part of black students, overstepped the bounds.

A black student, passing under the windows of the dorm where the footballers lived, was urinated on, supposedly by accident. When he remonstrated against the act, he was laughed at and jeered at by some of the ones who saw the incident. He "lost his cool" and went in after them. He was a well-built young man who knew how to take care of himself and in the ensuing brawl gave one of the footballers a severe going over. They chased him out of the dorm, and he ran over to the rooms of black students. In no time at all, a melee of the first order was under way. The campus police were called and in a short time had order restored.

Fortunately, by this time some of the members of the campus security force were black. One or two of them were on duty when the call came in, and they were on hand to take charge. Of course, the campus was buzzing the next day about the incident. One of the white students had charged that a knife had been drawn by one of the black students, and he claimed that he had been cut. A counter claim by the black students was that a white student had been seen with a half length of heavy chain wrapped around his fist, flailing away during the brawl.

The Dean of Students office and the Dean of the College office met to discuss the situation. The tone of the discussion was that black students may have gone too far and that some severe disciplinary measures would have to be taken against the offenders. Joe Moore, from the Dean of Students office, and I put in a disclaimer to that line and said that there was ample reason to believe that there had been undue provocation by the white students that had been building up to just such an incident. The fact that black students had not taken things into their hands before now was evidence that they were not out to seek trouble. There should be a thorough investigation of the whole scene, including the residential patterns of that part of the campus and the attitudes that existed. It was agreed that an investigation would be carried out and that the findings would be put before the university disciplinary committee.

During the days that followed, an interesting thing began to happen. Students whom I knew and didn't know began to come into my office and tell me of the things that they had experienced themselves or had witnessed–actions of a small number of students who had sworn to run black and non-American students off "their campus." I kept note of their statements and asked them if they would be willing to testify before the committee if it became necessary. Some demurred, but many of them said they would.

The picture that began to emerge was not pretty. It had long been a point of great annoyance to some of the "old timers" that the area around the student residences was unsightly with rubbish strewn about after the weekends. Beer cans and bottles, waste food, and other garbage were a common sight. Even some of the groundskeepers had complained about the lack of attention that students paid to the normal care of their surroundings. An inspection of some of the rooms in the residences brought to light the fact that some of them were filthy and made almost uninhabitable by the students who lived there. In one discussion with the administration, I termed the area the "Golden Ghetto" and stated that these were conditions that, on the outside, would have been condemned as the practice of the black, the poor, or the lower class. Living in conditions like these was conducive to the breakdown of all kinds of human values and relationships.

As chairman of the university Human Relations Committee, I had a clear opportunity to fire away at the laissez faire attitude that was taken towards students as people. Something would have to be done that would affect the whole campus and put things on a healthier level. Discriminatory attitudes, even subtle ones, would have to be declared unwelcome and subject to penalty should they continue. The rights of every student on the campus, regardless of color, would have to be emphasized and protected.

The disciplinary committee heard all of the evidence and in the end penalized both the black and white students who had been the principals in the affray. The white student objected to the findings of the committee and threatened to take the matter to the local court. No lawyer in the community would touch the case, and he finally let it drop. An important point still had to be made. The existing residential pattern had to be changed, and one be instituted to avoid grouping people into situations they could lay claim to as theirs. All rooms and quarters were open for bidding, and no person or group could maintain residence for more than a year at a time. Athletes could no longer be given special preference as groups in special areas of the campus. As was to be expected, there was great dissatisfaction from some quarters of the campus, but the administration was firm and unequivocal in its pronouncements and its statement of intent. Hopefully, the Golden Ghetto was on the way out.

The third development during this period was that a black studies program had been carefully prepared and introduced as part of the university's course offerings. We had taken note of some of the failings of black studies courses in other universities and were determined that we would not follow suit. It had to be academically defensible and productive for black students and the campus as a whole. No courses were relegated to "blacks only" although it was obvious that some of the courses would have little appeal to anyone who was not black. Above all, it could not be looked upon as an easy way for black students to rack up credits. They would have to work as hard in these courses as they did in any course that they took in other departments. I can remember the interest and amazement some members of an academic committee expressed when, at the end of a term, some black students were put in jeopardy because they had failed one of the courses in the black studies program. To the great credit of the black faculty that had been hired to conduct these courses, they were fair but unyielding in their demands that students who took the courses measured up to the standard of performance they had established.

The headquarters of the black studies program was a building on campus that had formerly housed some special education programs. It was an adequate interim building for the program, but soon the students were asking for a building that would provide more space and would represent a permanent feature for the campus. Again, because of the position I held, I had an opportunity to present the arguments for this move directly to those who would have to make the decision. The argument was simple and to the point. I stated that the "ownership" syndrome was synonymous with belonging for most Americans. Therefore, the demand that they were making for a center or place of their own was logically within the framework of the syndrome most Americans valued and strove to achieve. The fact that they were welcome to join other clubs or centers did not mitigate the fact that they wanted a place where others could be invited.

When the question was raised as to whether other minority students would also want a place of their own, I replied by telling them that they were slightly behind the times. Black students were joining with other minority groups on the campus, and the need was for a center that would be available to all members of the "third world."* A committee was formed to look into the possible sites on campus. In due time, a building was designated that would suit the purpose. Money was allocated for its renovation. The center was to be headed by a black administrator and run like other student

---

*After more than thirty years on the campus, the Third World Center was renamed the Carl A. Fields Center for Equality and Cultural Understanding, effective July 1, 2002.

organizations on campus with a composition of student and faculty advisors. I did not know it then, but that was to be one of the last administrative decisions that I would have a part in making for black and minority students and for Princeton.

Carl Fields, age 2,
in 1921.

Carl, age 12.

Carl's grandfather, the
Reverend Albert S.
Grayson, who lived and
preached in Trenton,
New Jersey.

Extended Fields family, circa 1935.

Photographs: Courtesy of Fields family.

Carl, 2nd from left, was the first black student to be captain of a St. John's University sports team. He was inducted into the St. John's Athletic Hall of Fame in 1988.

Carl, Batallion Sargeant Major, during World War II, received the Bronze Star in the Battle of Saipan.

Carl, pictured in the *Vincentian 1942*, was the first black student to be tapped for the Scull and Circle honor society at St. John's.

Top photograph by Joseph C. Consentino, St. John's University. Courtesy of *St. John's University Alumni Magazine* (Winter, 1969).
Bottom left photograph: Courtesy of St. John's University.
Bottom right photograph: Courtesy of Fields family.

Carl, right, with Brad Craig, who recruited him for Princeton University and became a lifelong friend.

Juanita Foster, left, with husband, Badi Foster, who was the first black student at Princeton to talk to Carl.

Carl, seated right, chatting with Princeton students.

Carl, right, with colleagues John Danielson, left, and Jim Barbour, center, walking across campus.

Top photographs: Courtesy of Fields family.
Bottom photographs by Joseph C. Consentino, St. John's University. Courtesy of *St. John's University Alumni Magazine* (Winter, 1969).

Vigil in front of Nassau Hall, honoring the memory of Martin Luther King, Jr. in 1968.

Bust of Frederick Douglass, sculpted by Inge Hardison, to honor recipients of the Frederick Douglass Award. On permanent display in Firestone Library, Princeton University.

Carl, center, at Association of Black Collegians' first dinner banquet with Paul Williams, left, and Deane Buchanan, right, first recipients of the Frederick Douglass Award in 1968.

Top left photograph: *Princeton Alumni Weekly*, April 30, 1968, p. 15.
Published with permission of Princeton University Library.
Top right photograph: Courtesy of Princeton University Library.
Bottom photograph: Courtesy of Fields family.

Carl, expressing his
views.

Carl, left, at job interview with K.D. Kaunda,
president of Zambia, center, and Lameck Goma,
vice-chancellor of University of Zambia, right.

Carl and wife, Hedda, just before
going to Zambia.

University of Zambia campus in 1970.

Photograph top left by Joseph C. Consentino, St. John's University. Courtesy of *St. John's University Alumni Magazine* (Winter, 1969).
Photographs top right and bottom left: Courtesy of Fields family.
Photographs bottom right: Courtesy of University of Zambia.

Carl, at home in New York City, with a mask from Zambia adorning the wall.

President William G. Bowen with Jerome Davis, Class of 1971 in the background, at the Tenth Anniversary Conference of the Association of Black Princeton Alumni in 1977.

Carl, back left, with brothers Ralph, Earl, and Sylvester. In front, father, Ralph, and mother, Queena.

Top photographs by Melvin R. McCray.
Bottom photograph: Courtesy of Fields family.

Carl, left, being given Honorary Doctor of Laws Degree from St. John's University by President Joseph T. Cahill in 1989.

Carl, left, after receiving medal of honor in 1997, with Donald J. Harrington, President of St John's University.

Left, Robert F. Goheen, President of Princeton University, 1957-1972, receiving the Carl A. Fields Memorial Service Award in 2000, with Harold Shapiro, President of Princeton University, 1988-2001, and Sergio Sotolongo, class of 1977, President of the Association of Black Princeton Alumni.

Top left photograph by Gene Luttenberg.
Top right photograph by Robert Floyd.
Bottom photograph by Devery Sheffield.

CARL A. FIELDS CENTER

Shirley Tilghman, President of Princeton University and Hedda Fields, at the renaming ceremony of the Third World Center as the Carl A. Fields Center for Equality and Cultural Understanding in 2002.

Robert F. Goheen and Hedda Fields at the renaming ceremony.

Photographs: Courtesy of the Fields family.

CHAPTER 7

HIRED—AFRICAN STYLE

By fall of 1970, I was well into my sixth year at Princeton. A growing number of black men and women had been moved into positions of prominence and authority in various fields. One of these was the Reverend Randolph Nugent, or Randy as he was called by most people, a Methodist minister who had been active in community organization programs and was now up top in the World Council of Churches. Randy called me at Princeton and asked if I could meet with him within the next day or so. I agreed and went to see him at his new offices at 475 Riverside Drive in New York. Someone had dubbed it "The God Box" because of the number of church organizations that occupied the premises.

Randy was concerned about the state of the missionary movement in Africa. It was his opinion that the movement was not keeping pace with the new African needs, and he asked me if I could develop a proposal that would focus on a new method of training missionaries for Africa. The intent would be to encourage more blacks to join forces with their counterparts in African states in order to seek a more relevant approach, through the church, to African development.

It sounded interesting, and in about two weeks I had written an outline proposal that we were able to discuss. We decided to ask about half a dozen other people whom I knew to come together and brainstorm the proposal. In the meantime, Randy was to check out the possible funding sources for the proposal in case it was approved by the board controlling mission activity.

Within a month or two, we had received the endorsement of the board, subject to further consideration as to the most positive site in Africa for such an undertaking. The consensus was that we ought to check out Central and East Africa. Four states were selected: Uganda, Kenya, Tanzania, and Zambia. Randy stated that there were good connections in each of the capital cities of Kampala, Nairobi, Dar es Salaam, and Lusaka.

Now, I was never a real student of Africa like some of the people I knew, but I had a long-standing interest in the so-called "dark continent." First, it was common knowledge in my family that great-great grandparents on both sides had been brought from Africa. Many of the anecdotes were concerned with how the "dumb" black slaves used their intelligence to outsmart the so-called "smart" plantation owners. I can remember sitting in history classes in elementary school and high school and wondering why the teacher didn't know that people in Africa weren't ignorant and savage as I did. Secondly, during my most impressionable younger years, I attended Abyssinian Baptist Church which, at that time, was pastored by Adam Clayton Powell, Sr., a giant of a man physically and mentally. The church supported black missionaries in Africa, and they came back at regular intervals, bringing with them African men and women who didn't have to have an interpreter and who could explain in clear English what they were all about. No matter what current black opinion thinks of the black church, it played an invaluable role in dispensing information about the truth of Africa and Africans.

Truth to tell, however, I had never had any burning urge to go to Africa just as I had no urge to go to Europe. The army has something to do with that. I had traveled whether I had wanted to or not, and now I was content to "see America first." It was with some surprise, therefore, that when the discussions began to turn on the question as to who should make this exploratory trip, I found myself wanting to be one of those selected. It all came about very naturally. I was the creator of the proposal. I was also the senior member of the group. My experience as an evaluator of educational programs and people was felt to be a necessary asset. So it was taken for granted that, if I could get the time from Princeton, I was to be one of the people to make the trip.

In addition to myself, there were Badi Foster and Jan Carew.* I had met Badi during my first year at Princeton. He had just begun graduate studies in political science and a chance meeting had ripened into a fast and enduring friendship. Jan was from Guyana, a man of broad experience and talent: an author, playwright, member of Nkrumah's educational advisory service, world traveler, and bon vivant. He had been brought to Princeton as a writer-in-residence. This was a ploy adopted from the white establishment that got a black man into a university when he was unable to satisfy the academic credential system. I had done my homework and had found out that there were a number of people on Princeton's payroll who couldn't play that game but were accepted because they had "exceptional talent" that rounded out the university community.

The period between Thanksgiving and Christmas was one of frantic activity for all three of us–shots, visas, travel arrangements, and getting out of Princeton. Family and close friends were told the

---

*Carew had personal contacts in the countries on the itinerary. Funding was secured from outside agencies, and the trip was not under the auspices of Princeton University. [Information provided by Badi Foster.]

purpose of the trip, but outside of that we kept things pretty close to the vest.

"A" day (Africa day) arrived and at about ten o'clock in the evening of the first of January, we were on our way. Our first stop was London where we expected to touch base and be filled in on the areas chosen, by Africans and Africanists. For me, names that I had read about began to take on presence–Kaunda, Nyerere, Obote, Kenyatta. We met people who knew what was currently happening. This was the first time that I realized that the information channels available to people in the United States about what was taking place in Africa were strictly censored. The average American, black or white, reads or hears what the State Department or other censoring media wants him to know. This is true not only for Africa but for other sectors of the world.

Finally, we were on our way to Africa and my first encounter with "the homeland." Now you can look at maps, see television clips, read all the articles you can lay your hands on, but there is nothing that prepares you for the vastness of the African continent. It is huge. When we deplaned at the international airport in Nairobi, I had mixed feelings of relief after a long flight and a rather objective interest in what I was moving into. Badi said, "This is Africa baby! Are you going to kiss the ground?" I said, "Hell no!" We both laughed. Jan was moving along with the sureness of the international traveler.

My first reactions were, "This is a hick airport for such an important city" and "My God, I've never seen so many black people outside of Harlem, the South side of Chicago, or Atlanta." As we entered the arrival building and I saw the health officials, customs officials, and all the other people that make an airport tick, I felt joyous. Okay. This is where it is. If that cat sitting in the booth says I don't come in, I don't come in. The first contact with nationhood. Power to the people? As I observed them going about their duties, it became obvious that this was not one of their hang ups. They were the people. They had the power. Enough said. As we cleared customs, the airport hustlers zeroed in on us. We were strangers and fair game. Baggage carriers and taxicab drivers around the world know no brotherhood based on color. It's all the same game. Get the pound, lire, kwacha, or whatever is the common currency. Make it. Make it.

On the way to the hotel, we engaged the driver in conversation. Except for his accent, he was like cab drivers the world over. Ready to talk about anything and everything. "First time in Nairobi?" "Yes." "Where are you from?" "The United States." Then came the "oh" with that particular rising inflection that we came to know as characteristic of Central and East Africans. A great sound that you have to hear to appreciate.

Once settled into the hotel, we began to make phone contact with the people who, we hoped, were expecting to see us. Now the excitement of being in Africa began to grip me. Walking the streets that evening, looking at the people with my kind of color, but all too conscious of the fact that I didn't know them and they didn't know me. Feeling, in a way, more strange than I did in London or than I would in some small town in the northern reaches of New England.

Within a day we had made contact with our man in the Nairobi office of The Ford Foundation, Will Lemelle, their only black Deputy Representative in Africa. This was the first of many clues that I was to pick up about our setup outside of the USA. "Hi man." "Hi brother." A black American in a 15'x 25' office, representing a piece of what we knew. The same language, the same awareness. Fill us in. Tell us what this is all about. Even Jan was eager to get the lowdown on what was happening.

In the midst of a thorough briefing on what the scene was like, Will suddenly began to talk about his problems in higher education

in that part of Africa and the extent to which positions in institutions were filled with one kind of person: white American. "By
God, I'd like to get a black guy into one of these institutions," he
exclaimed.* I was listening with interest, but with no particular
intent, to what he was saying. Then a direct question was put to
me. "What would it take to get you away from Princeton?" Hell! I
hadn't thought about it. Hold it. Yes, I had. For more than a year,
I had realized that the string was running out as far as my staying
at Princeton was concerned. Assistant Dean of the College.
Chairman of the Human Relations Committee. Privy to almost all
of the top policy decisions of the university, with especial concern
for minority groups. The most powerful black man on campus.
Lots of impact on the town-gown situation. Okay, so what next?
One article in the student newspaper had suggested that I could
become the successor to the presidency. Ha. Not yet. Not in my
lifetime! What else? What I knew I wanted, I wasn't going to get.
Moses standing on the mountain looking over into the Promised
Land. But that's it. And again...I ain't no Moses.

"It depends on what you've got to offer." Even as I said it, I knew
that I was open. Like the day I sat and talked to Brad when he came
on that rainy day to talk about Princeton. I could begin to feel
something. What followed was all matter-of-fact. I was going to
Zambia as part of this trip. Will would cable ahead and tell the vice-
chancellor that I would call for an appointment. The vice-
chancellor has asked Ford to find a person who could fill the bill as

---

*Prior to this trip to Africa, Lemelle, one of Foster's professors at the University of
Denver, had asked him to identify African Americans who might be interested in
working in African universities and be supported by Ford. Lemelle had met Fields as a
keynote speaker at the first ABC conference at Princeton. The rest of the trip became in
part one of job exploration at the University of Zambia. The fact that the trip was not
financed or sponsored by Princeton made it all right to broaden the purposes of the trip.
[Information provided by Badi Foster.]

Planning Officer for the university. Oh, the Princeton thing all over again. Okay, I'm up for that!

Lusaka, a different kind of African city. Clean, well laid out. The Ridgeway Hotel, turf of the former colonial rulers. Oh man. I contacted the office of the vice-chancellor the day after I arrived. He was busy, his secretary informed me. "Yes, but there should be a cable from Nairobi telling him that I would be calling." "Just a minute. Oh, yes. The vice-chancellor can see you on Thursday morning at ten o'clock." "Fine, I'll be there." Badi and Jan had begun to get into the act. "Man this is for you. We'll do all we can to see that it comes off." Enthusiasm. "Yeah, but hold it. I haven't seen this man yet. For all I know, we won't hit it off, and all this talk is for nothing. No sense in getting your hopes too high." "It's going to work," they said.

How do you dress for an interview with the head of a university out here? Is this any different from Princeton? Well, play it safe. Driving to the university in a private cab, I went over what the possible approaches could be. Might as well play it loose, I decided. The driver asked me about when I would want to return. I said to come back in about an hour.

Up the cement stairs. The campus was quiet, obviously on some kind of interim break. At the top of the stairway, I turned left into a waiting room. I saw an outer office and went in and announced myself. The secretary tapped on the connecting door and ushered me into the vice-chancellor's office. Coming towards me, with outstretched hand, was a smallish man, wearing a *chitenge* [African-patterned cotton shirt], eyeglasses framing a round face, partially bald, pants slightly baggy at the knees.

"This is the head of the university?" I said to myself. Then began the most absorbing hour and a half that I had ever spent in an interview. After a few amenities, the vice-chancellor, Professor L.K.H. Goma, launched into his vision of what an African university should be like, his hopes and desires for the University of Zambia, the need for advance planning, the frustration he had experienced working under expatriate heads in his own country, his desire to change what he had been subject to and make the university a viable and essential part of the building of the nation. When he had finished, I explained how I happened to be in that part of the world, the position I held at Princeton, what had been accomplished, the fact that a position such as he described would be something that I would like to take on, what I felt I could bring to the situation, and what I hoped I would learn from him and from others with whom I would be working, my limitations as to some of the requirements he had in mind, my expertise in certain areas that I was ready to put at his disposal. When I finished, there was a silence as we both looked at each other. It was like a mutual-encounter session. No holds barred and nothing left unbared that we both felt would make the situation clear for the next move.

"Right!" he said in that soft, modulated, African-British accent. "How soon could you start work? The job is yours if you want it." Without hesitation I responded, "I want it. I can be here by the first of August." "I'll write to the Ford office and tell them that you're the person I want. You take care of things there when you get back. If all works out, I'll expect you here in August." We rose and shook hands. Two black men from different parts of the world. Out of two different cultures. But he would accept my assistance, and I would share with him all that I had gained from experience.

As I descended the stairs and walked the short distance to the waiting cab, I murmured to myself, "Well, I'll be damned! I've got a job in Africa."

CHAPTER 8

THE BLACK ADMINISTRATOR—ANOTHER BEGINNING

The goodbyes to family and friends were over. Two stops between New York and Lusaka. Take off date between July 4th and July 14th. Independence Days. Yeah. Why not. Behind me were things I'd known; ahead of me were things I didn't know. What are you going to be independent of, man? Don't know! Don't know.

During the stopover in Dar es Salaam, I met another black American, Bill Sutherland, a professor at the university there. We had met in January. We exchanged greetings, and he asked what I was doing there this time. I told him of my appointment at the University of Zambia. He said, with a laugh, that I might not have a job to go to. I asked how come. He replied that the university had been closed because of a student riot. When? About a week before. A few more words between us with an invitation to visit him if I should get back to Dar in the future.

Student riot. Closed university. Well, there was certainly nothing to do but continue. I almost got held up at customs at the Lusaka International Airport because I did not have my copy of the work permit. I showed them the letter from the registrar of the university telling me to come ahead. The man in the booth was skeptical until the senior Ford Foundation consultant, Alan

Simmance, showed up and vouched for the authenticity of the letter and the position. Alan and I chatted on the way to the Inter-Continental Hotel, and he filled me in on the close down. No students were on campus, but all administrative personnel were still working. Did anyone know how long the close down would last? No.

Alan made a car available, and after a few days to rest up and get things together, I called the vice-chancellor and made arrangements to get to the university. He was as cordial as he had been the first time. I got a thorough briefing on the close down and the possible repercussions. He was in constant contact with all of the officials concerned and was expecting a call telling him of another meeting with them. There was nothing for me to do then. I made arrangements for a meeting later in the week. As I was about to leave, he said with a laugh, "Why don't you sign the guest register? This may be the last time you'll be in this office." I signed the register but said to myself, "Now just what in the hell does this mean?"

I had been trying to figure out how to arrange time for orientation, but here it was handed to me whether I wanted it or not. Hmm. So what else is new? I found out in short order. The house I was to occupy was not ready because of the interruption of the close down. The office I was to occupy was not ready because of the close down. And nobody was ready for me because of the close down. Mental note: you're not in Princeton any more. Stay loose.

Loose I was and loose I stayed for fifty-three days. The close down lasted for two months. It was three weeks later that I got an office and a week more before I occupied the house. In the interim I had time to acquaint myself with the environs. The campus setting was as unlike Princeton as you could get. The buildings on the Princeton campus are covered with ivy that softens the hard edges of stone or brick and cement. Trees abound and shrubs of all kinds are all over the place. The University of Zambia was a collection of solid, gray concrete buildings. At the time they were unrelieved by any substantial amount of greenery. Raw and stark in their severity against the skyline, set back about a quarter of a mile from the Great East Road, they created a feeling of remoteness. "By God," I said to myself, "A person comes here to get an education, and they make sure he is aware of that."

I began to bone up on the facts and statistics. The University of Zambia (UNZA, as it is called) was just over five years old. The student body was 95 percent Zambian, five percent non-Zambian. About 34 nationalities were represented on the faculty with better than two-thirds from European- or English-style universities. The vice-chancellor was the second vice-chancellor of the university and the first Zambian. Under him the top administrators were non-Zambian with 50 percent being white Europeans. From junior administrator level down, everyone was Zambian. There was a university council of which all but three or four members were Zambian. The chairman of the council was appointed by the president of Zambia who was also the chancellor of the university. The deans of all six schools of the university were white expatriates. Nine-tenths of the heads of subjects were white expatriates. The offices of resident engineer, resident architect, and horticulturalist were headed by white expatriates. The catering officer was from Ghana, an African woman. About the only thing African about UNZA was its location. Here I was, a black American, university planning officer!

The term "expatriate" had little or no meaning to me before I came to Zambia. I don't ever remember hearing it used in the States. But it didn't take long for me to understand its meaning and implication. If you are not a Zambian, you're an expatriate. Color is not a factor. If you are not Zambian, you are a "guest" of the nation. Like any guest, if you observe the rules, regulations, and procedures laid down by the governing bodies or the society, you are welcome to stay and do business. If you don't, you are declared persona non grata and asked to leave the country. The term here is "P.I." or "prohibited immigrant." I've heard of and known a few people, black and white, who got "P.I.'d." Believe me, it is a sobering concept and reality. One can claim brotherhood, sisterhood, cousinhood, or even fatherhood, but if you're not native to the country and run afoul of the established rules of the government, being black is no help. Blackness, all shades and conditions of it, is an accepted fact of the society. Your acceptance as an individual or member of a group in the society is based on merit, what you do and how well you do it; on your acceptance and awareness of objectives of government and how closely you support and adhere to them; on you as a person and your ability to relate positively to other people.

Once this was clear to me, I made no attempt to parlay blackness per se into privilege or an asset. I was an experienced administrator who was expected to do a thorough, professional job for the university. I was an American, like it or not. That was my problem! I had to make it as a person with whatever knowledge or skill I possessed in the area of interpersonal relationships. That's the way it was, and that's the way it is. When a British professor mentioned the fact that I was probably the first black American planning officer in any African university, I really could say, "So what?"

I think it is interesting to consider the factors that led to the closing down of the university. France had just completed an agreement with South Africa that would provide arms and other strategic military items. The reaction of the students at UNZA was vehement. They marched to the French Embassy with petitions to protest the agreement. Windows and some other property at the Embassy were damaged. President Kaunda had issued a strong condemnation of the pact between France and South Africa. A group of about ten students published a letter to the president condemning the "mildness" of his statement and making some remarks which could be (and were) construed as disrespectful to the president. The reaction of the Cabinet was swift. Elements of the military were ordered to the campus to find the offending students and close down the university. This was done without prior consultation with the vice-chancellor or other responsible administrative authorities. The faculty proclaimed the sanctity of academic freedom and protested its abridgment. The reply of the government was that academic freedom could be tolerated as long as it did not defy stated government policy and the person of the president. The students were called "irresponsible and ungrateful." The educational opportunities they enjoyed were sponsored solely by the government. Since they acted like "bad children," they would be treated like "bad children."

The ten ringleaders were jailed, tried and subsequently found guilty of endangering the safety of the state and defamation of character as far as the president was concerned. The ten students submitted a public apology to the president who accepted it. They would not serve a prison sentence but would be denied return to the university for one year. Every other student had to reapply for re-entrance to the university and was required to sign a statement that prohibited any future action of this nature.

The vice-chancellor and chairman of the university council made a stout defense of the right of open expression and strongly requested that no action by military or police be taken against the institution or its students without prior consultation. They won their point. The president, who is also chancellor of UNZA, reconciled government and university by attending and speaking at the first university council meeting held after the close down.

By the time the university had begun to settle into something of its normal pattern, things sped up. During the close down, the university had been spinning its wheels while the vice-chancellor and his staff focused on resolving the situation. Now two or three months work had to be done in one, and the planning officer was plunged, without ceremony, into the thick of things. It was an interesting experience to say the least.

My projected date with the vice-chancellor had not taken place because of the priority of another meeting connected with the crisis. It wasn't until after classes had resumed that I was able to meet with him for an extended period of time and discuss the factors of the job I was to handle. He wasted no time. The Ministry of Education had rejected the five-year budget based on student, staff, and capital figures which had been submitted. They needed new projections within a period of three or four weeks so they could present the total budget for educational needs to the Parliament. My assignment: recast the figures and the budget. I would be assigned one of the professors who had been at the university from the beginning and who had a wealth of knowledge that would be helpful.

With a copy of the rejected budget in hand, I retreated to my office where I had finally gotten a desk, chair, and lamp and began to pore over it. I highlighted the information I needed to have and began to hunt for a phone to begin business. Oh yes. There was no phone in my office because the General Post Office, which handles those things, was still dickering with the university about the need for extra lines. The nearest phone was down the hall in a busy office, and I had to wait my turn to use it. If that was too busy, I had the option of going across to the administration building, and trying to find the bursar's, registrar's, or even the vice-chancellor's phone, and using one of them.

The computers at the university could only provide limited

assistance since they were not set up to handle administrative data. Alan Ward, a fine physics professor and equally fine person who had been assigned to help me, provided some figures and statistics that he had been gathering. He also recommended that I contact the Ministry of Education for assistance with secondary-school projections for the next five years. Fortunately, during my orientation period, I had met a former Ford Foundation consultant, Trevor Coombe. Trevor was a former member of the School of Education at UNZA, and was now with the Ministry of Education as a director of planning. We had hit it off from the beginning because of our Ivy League affiliation. He was a Harvard Ph.D., and we could talk the same language. I had asked him if he would mind my using his background and experience in Zambia as a means of developing a stronger liaison with the planning functions at UNZA. He said he would welcome the closer association between the university and ministry. So, without hesitation, I put this to the test.

It worked. Trevor supplied all the data and statistics his office had on projected graduates from the secondary sector over the next five-year period. By combining university senate minutes and any other information I had found, I began to put together a picture of what the future might look like numbers wise. Then I was ready to put it all together, or so I thought.

As an American, I turned to the automated objects, with which we are so familiar, to put things together and work out the details of the figures. "Ah ha, Fields. You don't learn too fast, do you? Where do you think you are? Princeton or someplace like it?" Three of the four calculating machines, including the one in the vice-chancellor's office, were out of order. The operative one could not be spared. What to do? What to do? Pencil and paper, of course. But this is a thirty-five million dollar budget, and it has to be accurate. Student numbers and faculty positions have to jibe with capital development projections or else the whole thing is a waste. The last time this was done, it was handled by a committee; this time it's being prepared and presented by the planning officer. Dig? I dig.

It had taken two weeks of the four-week deadline that the vice-chancellor had set for me to obtain everything I could. Running from deans' offices to ministry offices. Following up any leads that were offered as to where I could find or dig out information. Now I had to put it together, the hard way as far as I was concerned. Put it together I did. For five days and most of the nights, I lost decimal points and found them. I read and re-read figures before I put them down, and, when they were added up, they didn't add up. I cursed, I prayed. At one point I was ready to get drunk and forget the whole damned thing!

But I remembered an incident that had taken place during my college days. At the end of my freshman year I got a job in the Catskills as a waiter and busboy. They told me that the money was good, and I'd be earning about $150 to $200 per week at this hotel. My mother didn't like the idea for a number of reasons. Chiefly, she said that it was hard work, and I had not done anything like that before. I pooh-poohed her reasoning since I had just come off a hard track season and was in good condition. She said, "Well, if it gets too hard, you can always come home."

For the first two weeks before the season, I worked 19 hours a day and earned $50 a week. I was bone tired and told the manager that if this was what he called good money, I was getting out. A friend of mine suggested I think it over and give it a longer try. I told him that I really didn't have to work that hard for such little money; I could go back home and make that much doing almost nothing. Then my mother's words came back to me. I decided that if I dropped dead, I wasn't going back home admitting that she had been right and the job was too hard for me. Now, if I couldn't admit that to my mother, you know I wouldn't admit it to the vice-chancellor. I submitted the finished product three days ahead of the deadline. There were a few things I had found out about the hierarchy of central administration. First there was the vice-chancellor. Then there was a pro-vice-chancellor who was an academic who assisted with certain routine administrative duties when the vice-chancellor was absent. Next in the direct line of authority came the registrar and under him, but with his own sphere of influence, came the bursar. As planning officer, I was between the vice-chancellor and the registrar, responsible only to the vice-chancellor

The African and African-related expatriate is very status conscious. Oftentimes, they pay respect to the position first and the man second. I was in a power position. But like any power position, there are disadvantages if it isn't handled properly. The African might not pay attention to color, but the expatriate European might. I was too new to make even temporary enemies. The bursar was an expatriate from England who had been in several African universities. He was basically an accountant who had worked his way up to the position of bursar as others had left. He had an indefatigable capacity for work and was intensely loyal to the vice-chancellor.

The day after I submitted the budget projections to the vice-chancellor, I paid a visit to the bursar and dropped a copy on his desk. He took a quick look at it and asked me who had told me to do it. I replied that the vice-chancellor had told me to handle it because he, the bursar, was busy with something else that was very important. That really was a shot in the dark, but it worked. He muttered something about people who didn't know his work being given it without his say so. I gave way on this point but said that when the vice-chancellor asked you to do something, you could hardly refuse. We reluctantly agreed. I then asked him if he would do me a favor and check over the figures because I was sure I had missed something and I couldn't find it. I told him that figures were really not my strength, and I'd be grateful if he found the error before the vice-chancellor.

I could tell from his expression that I was on target. He said that he'd check them out and see me in a day or two. He was in the next morning and explained to me where the mistake had been made. I complimented him on a sharp eye and asked him why I hadn't seen the same thing. He said, with a smile, there were some things that only he knew concerning the finances of the institution, and I couldn't be expected to know them since I was so new to the university.

CHAPTER 9

IN COMMON CAUSE

It has already been mentioned that being black in Africa earns you no merit badges or unusual distinctions. It is, therefore, for most black Americans, a different kind of experience. Strange as it may sound, I found this almost a relief. The emphasis was and is on ability. If you're black with ability, so much the better. No ability and it doesn't make any difference what color you are. You're not a preferred person in most instances. The days when a mediocre expatriate European or American could hold an important position in various national and para-statal organizations is rapidly coming to and end. I hope that their places will not be filled with equally mediocre Africans. Progress in nation building would be substantially impaired.

The main difference between an old university and a new one is the nature and adequacy of its infrastructure, plus the quality and quantity of the people available to operate it. In Zambia, at Independence 1964, less than one hundred Zambians had bachelor's degrees. The quality was there, but the quantity was and still is slim. The designers of the university sought to compensate for this by vesting most basic policy decisions in the university council. The chief executive, the vice-chancellor, did no more than carry out the policies decided upon by the council. This might have been adequate at the beginning, but by 1971 it had begun to show its weaknesses and disadvantages. The incumbent vice-chancellor had been quick to perceive this and had already begun to develop measures that would correct the situation. The position of planning officer was one of these measures.

Now it's one thing to go into a place like Princeton new to the surroundings and practices, but it's quite something else at a place like UNZA. At Princeton, you have access to resources in the immediate surroundings, an hour or two away, or at the very least within telephone range. At UNZA, as you might guess, you have yourself. That makes it a different kind of a ball game. The burden of proof is on you. The defining of the position, what it can do, what it should do, what it should become. Most of all it is overcoming the antipathy that many people have, outside of the United States, to an American, black or white.

I can remember with clarity the impression and comment of a fellow American after my first Senate meeting. Ed Lawson was the dean of the School of Engineering at the time. He and his wife, Mary, had been most helpful to my wife and me during our initial days in Lusaka. Ed was the kind of guy who made it a point to know all the ropes and would then pass the information on to anyone that he knew was strange to the situation.

At this meeting, an issue was raised that I later found out had been in the balance between academic procedures and administrative procedures. At the end of a lengthy discussion, the vice-chancellor turned to me and asked if I had anything to contribute. As a matter of fact I did, but I had already determined that this was not the time nor the place. Therefore, I said I was too new to the situation to give an opinion.

Within a few minutes the meeting was adjourned. In the corridor Ed rushed up to me and shook my hand with extreme fervor. "By God," he said, my heart was in my mouth. "I thought you were going to come off like a typical American know-it-all and say the wrong thing. Am I glad that you said nothing. That topic was loaded." In such fashion does one establish a reputation for considered deliberation.

Shortly thereafter, when my office was finally furnished with everything except a phone, and people had begun to find out where I was located, I began to have a steady stream of callers. Was I going to do something about the inefficiency of the various administrative units of the university? Yes, I hoped so. Was I in charge of providing blackout shades for rooms? No, I was not. Office space for academics was in short supply; was I going to see to it that this was remedied? Yes, I would look into that situation and recommend a procedure. What the hell did a planning officer do anyway? I'll tell you as soon as I find out myself.

Certain factors about the university began to stand out immediately. First, there are a hell of a lot of people from Europe, the U.K. and commonwealth countries, and the United States who have made the new nations of Africa their shopping ground. They get into new universities that have money and use them as vehicles for trying out their ideas or as a means of finishing up some part of a well-worked thesis that they pass off as new to an institution that is looking for status and recognition in the "accepted" academic world. Some of them are sincere and dedicated people who really seek to aid the development of new universities in Africa or anywhere else. Most of the others would appear to be parasites of the academic world, feeding on new situations until they are caught, and then they disappear.

UNZA has about two million dollars worth of obsolete equipment, ordered by "specialists" who stayed less than two years, lying idle in a storage room. They trained no one in its use while they were there, and in most cases it can't be traded off to the countries or areas from which it came. A new breed of "robber barons" or, as some of my African friends say, a new form of neo-colonialism.

Second, is the anxiety, amounting almost to a neurosis, the African has about whether his degree from a native institution has credibility among westernized universities. The tendency to emulate Oxford, Cambridge, Harvard, Yale, Princeton, or the other "ten best colleges or universities" of the western world has had a tremendous effect until recently.

Third, is what I consider the healthiest and most authentic movement in African higher education, concern about what we need to do in order to make the products of our institutions relevant to our society and our needs. It is this last trend of thought that, to me, gives an indication of what the African university should be about: to make a relevant, pragmatic, and logical tool of progress and development. In addition, it should seek to give to education a spiritual tone that gives to man his rightful place at the center of human effort.

Now obviously a planning officer should develop a plan of operation in his own mind first before he trots it out for anyone else to look at. My terms of reference called for paying attention to the academic, administrative, and physical development phasing of the university over a ten-year period. My experience taught me that the hardest group to do anything with in terms of change is the pure academic type. The institution of higher education is their turf, and they guard it with a fervor equal to that of any street gang that I used to work with. Experience has also taught me that the most vulnerable part of any organization is its administrative operation. I knew that I was going to have to come through the back door when it came to physical development, so I decided to zero in on the administration of the university as my first target.

It was fairly easy to ascertain what had taken place in the early development of the institution. The first chief administrators had been caretakers of university development. Very few people knew what had gone into the nature of decisions that had or had not been made. Very little was written down that would give clues to the operations. The people who had succeeded them had to pick up what was there and then try to sort out, as best they could, the various operations that were essential to good administration.

I felt it was necessary to establish a premise from which all other action would flow. The accepted motto of the university was "Service and Excellence." I took off from there and reasoned that the university was a service agent of the country. To carry out this role with the greatest efficiency, the university had to establish excellence in service internally in order to support the other functions of the university, i.e., educational services. We should, therefore, develop a method by which we could evaluate the administrative services of the university and determine the nature of the priorities that would result in their improvement. The premise was accepted.

The next step was to develop a unit I could act through without being too visible. It was better, I reasoned, to act through a group established as a university entity with authorized powers than to act on my own behalf as a planning officer, a person whose function nobody understood.

I discussed this with the vice-chancellor, and he agreed to set up a vice-chancellor's committee with broad terms of reference enabling the committee to look into matters, recommend action, and carry out the action with a minimum of red tape. Any action we conceived that might have policy implications, the committee was to refer to the vice-chancellor for his consideration and action. The committee was called the University Services Committee–a very proper title, and one that offered me all the protection I would need for the time being.

Each of the members of this committee had certain powers and authority that he could use in the normal conduct of business. The chief annoyance, irritation, and frustration of the expatriate centered around his lack of authority in an independent manner. A common complaint was that expatriates could not fire or dismiss a person who they felt was lazy, negligent, or hostile. All action had to be referred to an appropriate disciplinary unit in which they had no faith. Their lack of ability to "go it alone" and get things done was leading to a kind of apathy and hopelessness that was harmful to the Zambian employees and to themselves.

The committee was formed and included all of the top non-academic officers of the university. This was an important ploy. The academic side of the university had its full complement of committees and boards that took care of academic matters. The administration had nothing to take care of its needs. The academic side had the full recognition of the university as an action body. The administration had nothing to act as a validation of its importance. The vice-chancellor appointed me as chairman of the committee, and the stage was set.

Some of the members of the committee had been a part of the first administration. The rest had been brought in under the new administration. I had developed a list of what I considered to be essential university services. These were presented to the group for amendment, change, or, if necessary, complete reconstruction.

Looking at the group, I decided to use some of my group-work skills and get them to tell me what they thought was wrong and how things could be put right. Again, I hit the right approach. Instead of coming off as the big-shot planner, I was engaging them in the beginning of a planning process which they would help to develop and thus would help to implement. I was almost snowed under by the information that began to flow from their accumulated experience.

Once they had talked it out, relieving themselves of the irritations, annoyances, frustrations, and anything else they chose to put on the table, I suggested that they each produce a paper detailing the services that should be improved. We would all read each paper and together try to work out solutions to the problems presented. We would also establish a set of priority items that would focus the attention of the other areas of the university on our work.

One of the things we knew we had to do was not only formulate a plan of action but make sure that the plan was implemented. Even though the group was willing to participate, there was no real faith in the fact that anything we produced would be put into effect. Each person had had the experience of trying to put ideas into action on his own without much success. It was essential to prove that what one person could not achieve on his own could be achieved by group effort.

I needed a test case, and I got it quite by accident. The advanced medical students had been situated on a campus close to the university teaching hospital. Their being isolated from the main student body had caused some minor problems. The Department of Extramural Studies used the same campus for conferences and meetings stemming from their programs. Since some of the conferences brought people together from outside Lusaka, sleeping quarters had been set up to avoid unnecessary travel and disruption of conference proceedings.

These sleeping areas had recently been renovated by the department at its own expense. About the same time, a decision was made to renovate some of the rooms of the medical students. In order to minimize inconvenience to them, they were moved temporarily into the newly renovated sleeping quarters of the Extramural Department. This had taken place just before I arrived on the scene.

It so happened that the director of the Extramural Studies

Department was a member of the University Services Committee. At a meeting where we were discussing space allocations and needs, he stated that he was in need of additional space. He explained that the quarters that had been renovated for the use of the department were in the possession of about 25 medical students and that they had refused to move back to their own rooms even after they had been redecorated.

The dean of students, who was also a member of the committee, said that he knew about the problem, and it was very touchy. He had tried to get the students to return to their rooms, but they had almost manhandled him during one of a series of hot discussions. The vice-chancellor had met with a special student delegation in an effort to resolve the problem, but the students had been adamant. The situation had been allowed to lie dormant for almost a year.

The reason for the student attitude needs some explanation. The students knew that the need for qualified Zambian doctors was critical. They would be among the first to graduate and take up posts in various parts of the country. Since they were going to assume positions of such importance, they reasoned that they should have the best accommodations the university could provide. Comfort was essential to study. In other words, they were adopting the "elite" status they hoped to become accustomed to.

Several proposals were discussed, but finally the committee agreed that the students should return to their original quarters. In trying to determine how this decision should be transmitted to the students, I discovered that there was no policy statement on record that spelled out the rights and responsibilities of the university governing the use of its property or its space. This was inconceivable to me.

I went back to my office and proceeded to develop a memorandum to the vice-chancellor that would set forth the sovereignty of the university in this and all other areas of a similar nature. The vice-chancellor accepted it and issued an official statement of the principles. It was distributed to all parts of the university community.

The dean of students was then instructed by the committee to write a letter to the students informing them that the provisions of the statement were to be put into effect immediately. The students asked him to attend a special meeting. The dean was told not to make any concessions or agree to any compromises that might be put to him in the meeting. He was a representative of the committee and was to inform the students that, since the committee had made the decision, only the committee had the power and authority to reverse the decision.

The students tried to appeal the decision to the vice-chancellor. He refused to see them or discuss the matter, saying that the decision was that of the committee and that he could not overrule a committee that he had constituted and given authority to in matters like this.

The students threatened to take the case to the press. This caused some concern because the university was trying to overcome the bad publicity occasioned by the shutdown a year earlier. I advised them against telling the students not to take the story to the press. I suggested that the effect would be just the opposite of what they had in mind. They would be publicly accused of trying to develop an elitist status, and this was in direct opposition to the statements of the government and the party.

The committee stood firm. The students stood firm. I asked for a meeting with the vice-chancellor, the registrar, and the dean of students. The vice-chancellor instructed the registrar to prepare a letter to be sent to the recalcitrant students, giving them 72 hours to leave the temporary quarters and return to their own or face expulsion from the university because they were in violation of a university policy and regulation. The dean was instructed to inform the students that they would be receiving the letter. The letter was sent.

In the next meeting of the committee, the dean of students reported that the students had left the premises within 48 hours after receipt of the letter and ultimatum. The committee was delighted. We had won an important first victory and established the fact that we could not only plan but execute the plan. It was a great boost to morale and confidence in the group process.

The word began to get around that the University Services Committee was a force to be reckoned with. The members of the committee were their own best advertisement. They began to refer to the work of the committee and the importance it had for the campus community. Naturally, the academic sector began to wonder if they had anything to worry about. They soon had an answer.

The capital and recurrent budgets submitted by the university had been severely cut back due to the poor financial circumstances the government found itself in with the drop in the price of copper on the world market. This had resulted in the vice-chancellor informing us that economies would have to be made in every sector of the university. It was up to the University Services Committee to make the recommendation that would act as a guide for the vice-chancellor This was the opening I had been waiting for. I now had an opportunity to deal directly with the academic community, but again, not out of my own hat, but as chairman of the University Services Committee.

CHAPTER **10**

CRISIS IN BLACK—ANOTHER DIMENSION

From 1963 to the end of the decade, any black man who chose to go into administration in an American educational institution that was predominantly white was in a seller's market. He had options which hitherto he could not exercise. When he was asked how long he was going to stay with the institution, he could legitimately say, "I don't know." It depended on how he assessed the situation and how responsive he thought it would become to the needs of black students and black administrators.

In retrospect, I can see very clearly how my attitude differed from those of my white colleagues who wound up as administrators at Princeton. They had arrived at "Mecca" in terms of a position. To me it was an opportunity that had come later than it should have and that I could move away from if something more challenging came along.

In Africa, the situation is quite different. You are not native to the country or the situation. You are brought in under contract like everyone else who is not native to the country. You have a limited period of service, determined not by you, but by the organization with whom you have the contract, or by the needs of the government that you are brought in to assist. This comes as a shock to most Afro-Americans who carry with them the mystique of common heritage and brotherhood that, in the United States at least, is supposed to give you "common cause" on an automatic basis with your African "brother" or "sister." That ain't the way it is!

Africa is one of the great transient population areas of the world. If you are not a native, you're transient in one way or another. Most people know this and treat it as a natural condition. As a black American, you are stripped of much of your optional behavior, like other nationals. If you don't say it yourself, there are ways for people who are interested to find out how long you're going to be around. In a university setting this is important information. It determines whether people feel that they have to take you seriously or not.

In a situation where transience of personnel is a given, the planning process can be a mixed blessing. If you're not going to be there long enough to have to deal with all that it may imply, you can accept it and welcome it as a necessary ingredient of progress. If you're going to have to live through the transition that planning may imply, it's a threat to the even tenor of your ways.

The task of the planning officer, therefore, is two-dimensional in the university: first, setting up the plans that will affect the university of the future; and second, dealing with the attitudes and responses of the personnel, both transient and native, that will be affected by those plans in the present and in the future. There is a very intimate relationship between the two factors.

The person who is key to anything that is done administratively or academically in universities in Africa is the vice-chancellor. He also has an important effect on the physical development side. It's important to know something about this office. In most African countries, there is only one national university. This creates a situation wherein the position of vice-chancellor can be either strictly academic, strictly political, or a combination of the two. In any case, the vice-chancellor is always in contact with the political forces of the country because the institution is a product of and subject to the political forces and powers in government. A parallel in the United States is the state university. The important difference is that which accrues to being the only university in the nation as against being one of a number of state universities in a republic like the United States.

Very early on, I had decided that it was important for me to develop a close contact and relationship with the vice-chancellor. After all, he was my boss. I was there to carry out his ideas as to what the university of the future should be like. It could be a challenging and interesting experience on both a personal and professional level. The vice-chancellor was reputed to be one of the finest scientists in Africa. A Cambridge Ph.D., he was one of that small number of Zambians who had been consultants to the commission that had created the university. As the first Zambian vice-chancellor, he was very conscious of the responsibility that was his in developing an educational process that would be of benefit to the country. He brought to the position the same careful inquiry that he would use in the development of a research problem in his discipline.

From the discussions we had, it became evident that we shared a common concern: the development of an African university. The universities in English-speaking Africa had been developed on the basis of the western model out of either the U.K. or the U.S. The only thing African about them was their physical location. It was beginning to be evident that this model was no longer consonant with the needs and aspirations of developing African nations. The problem was, and is, how to reconstitute the university so that it reflects through its educational process the aims, needs, and priorities essential to the developing nation. Also, in doing this, how to maintain the high caliber of the educational content so that its students would be on a par with those of other societies and educational institutions throughout the world.

With the global understanding of the dilemma facing universities in Africa, our specific problem was how to meet and deal with it at the University of Zambia. The vice-chancellor decided that the first target would be the School of Education. One of the mandates that the university had been given was that of producing more Zambian teachers and administrators for the secondary school system. Eighty-five percent of the existing teachers were expatriates. The cost of maintaining this situation, both in terms of money and quality of instruction, was exorbitant.

The School of Education, as it functioned, was almost literally the product of the energy of one man. As an educationist, he had gained the respect and confidence of persons high up in the Ministry of Education and the Zambian government. From this position he was able to carry on the development of the school unilaterally with his own ideas and perceptions. He was charismatic, intelligent, shrewd, and, according to his close friends, could talk the white off a billiard ball. In African terms, he was an "empire builder." The School was set up along the lines of the English model with a Department of Education, an Institute of Education, and a Science Education Center. The faculty complement contained no Zambians and only two Africans, who were about to leave. Just before I had arrived, the "prime mover" of the school had left to take up another post in Africa.

There was no doubt about the vice-chancellor's position. The School of Education was not fulfilling expectations. If it could not be restructured to meet the demands of the nation and the expectations of the university, it would be eliminated altogether and a fresh start would be made. I felt a little like the man who picks up the destructible tape at the beginning of the television serial, "Mission: Impossible." "Your task, Mr. Planning Officer, should you choose to accept it, is to find a way to restructure the School of Education." I chose to accept it.

The next few months were spent in painstaking research of the School of Education. Where did its personnel come from? How long were they going to stay? What was its relationship to other parts of the university? What did other professionals think of its operation? Who was the new dean? What ideas did he have about the school and its objectives? What about the ministry? Was it satisfied with what the school was doing? These and other relevant questions were posed, and the answers began to give me the picture I needed along with a possible plan that would result in the restructuring of the school.

I took the plan of action to the vice-chancellor and laid it out for his approval. Elimination of the school and a new start would be disruptive and costly. Restructuring it was the logical approach. Agreed. I proposed that the vice-chancellor constitute a blue-ribbon panel to develop recommendations for the restructuring of the school. The panel would consist of representatives from the School of Education and university schools most closely related to the School of Education—Humanities and Social Sciences and the Natural Sciences. Most importantly, the panel would include representatives from the Ministry of Education who were Zambians and other Zambians well known for their interest in and contribution to education in Zambia. The vice-chancellor would give the charge to the panel with instructions to present its findings and recommendations to him for approval and implementation.

A list of names was prepared and presented to the vice-chancellor for amendments or deletions, and invitations were sent out. I offered the chairmanship of the panel to the dean of the School of Education. He refused. The vice-chancellor then appointed the planning officer as chairman. It was my ball game to win or lose.

I think I have mentioned before that a large part of my training had been in the area of counseling, both with individuals and groups. I had long since found out that individuals do not act the same way in group situations as they do alone. This is basic and essential background for any administrator who is going to be working with individuals as members of group situations.

For instance, the person who is loudest in his denunciation of a proposal in individual, face-to-face contact, is not necessarily going to give vent to the same feelings in a group situation unless the climate is right. This does not mean that he doesn't have the same convictions, but that against other unknowns he is more cautious and self-protective in his statements. The task of a chairman or group leader, therefore, is to make the known factors readily available to the group. Group confidence can be established through individual contributions to the known factors that support, in a real way, the ability of the group to move into discussions or considerations of unknown factors. Most important of all is to realize that the chairman or group leader is both a known and unknown factor to the group.

During my period of observation and information gathering, I had already ascertained that there were nuances of agreements and understandings between expatriates in various positions. Within reason, there was a kind of loose collaboration to protect and maintain the status quo whenever possible. All other things considered, this is a natural state of affairs. The important unknown to me was the Zambian contingent on the panel. I was aware that, as against other expatriates on the panel with whom they were more familiar, I was the unknown quantity. On the other hand, I had been selected for the position of planning officer and chairman of this panel by a Zambian whom they respected and knew to be uncompromising in his search for quality as it affected the welfare of the

University of Zambia. Stalemate.

The strategy to use was laid out in my mind. First, to have a clear and comprehensive picture of what the School of Education had been doing and was presently doing to meet the needs of the nation for trained secondary school teachers. Second, to examine the methods and processes used to determine if they would meet the exigencies of the next decade. If the present system and structure were deemed inadequate, then the way would be open to entertain and assess new measures that would ensure that goals would be met. This should entail consideration of the kind of structure that would make these new methods and processes viable and feasible.

I was also counting heavily on one other factor. As I have stated, the School of Education was a one-man enterprise in which Zambians had little or nothing to say about policy or procedure. My hunch was that if the present system was patently unequal to the task before it, the Zambians would welcome the opportunity to shape a school that would cater to their ideas and their understanding of its needs. In the end, it would be theirs to promote and work with in order to ensure success.

It may be important to state at this point the obvious difference between an institution like Princeton and one like UNZA. By and large, Princeton enjoys and has built a reputation for excellence in education that almost all who work there or become a part of attempt to implement or promote. The University of Zambia is in the process of attempting to build a reputation for excellence in education for the present and the future. As I have stated before, they are mainly dependent upon a transient, contracted group of expatriates. As a transient group they bring a broad diversity of ambition and interest to the university. There is, as yet, no unifying objective that motivates them to take a position at the university. This is especially true of those members of the faculty who represent 80 to 85 percent of faculty positions, expatriates all.

It was this diversity of motivation and ambition that made the panel a challenge. Were they working for themselves alone, or were they working toward an attitude and a level of performance that would promote pride in the institution and what it was able to do? Could they form the building blocks of a new school that they could look back on with pride, or would they perpetuate the myth that African nations and universities could never amount to anything much because they were deviating from traditional methods and procedures? It was almost a question of the old missionary ethic. Do you come to reform the "savages" and introduce them into the methods of salvation? Or do you come to learn how through their ideas, dreams, and desires you can promote their concept of a better social order and civilization?

The representatives from the School of Education were British and, in the main, were content to make minimal alterations in the school as long as they did not jeopardize their jobs and their understanding of what a School of Education was supposed to be about.

The dean of the School of Humanities and Social Sciences was an American whose sense of being in on the building of a new enterprise came out of a deep interest in people, stemming from her long involvement in social work and her belief that UNZA could be a place to be proud of now and in the future.

The dean of the School of Natural Sciences was an unorthodox Australian who, unable to put many of his ideas to work in his native environment, had taken a position as a biologist at the university in order to broaden his own learning and then had been made dean.

The other European expatriate was from the Ministry of Education, and his main objective was to make sure that the desires of the ministry, in the area of secondary school teacher production, were not hampered nor neglected.

The last European expatriate was a dedicated Africanist in the area of history whose reputation throughout the continent and in Zambia was impeccable. Indeed, he had been chosen as first pro-vice-chancellor by the relatively new Zambian vice-chancellor.

The director of extramural studies was Sudanese, seconded to the university because of his expertise in this field, a man with a deep belief in the future of all African universities and their effect on a growing, needful population.

The Zambian representative of the Ministry of Education was a long-time civil servant. His basic allegiance was to Zambia. His basic training had been under the colonial era of educational influence. He was prepared to go with that as long as it produced what Zambia needed and wanted. But he was not sure that the "system" was producing what he had in mind.

The principal of the teachers-training college, with which the School of Education was working, was conscious of the fact that change of a substantive nature, could endanger the enterprise he was heading. He was open and playing it both ways because he was determined not to come out as a "loser."

The other Zambian was a sophisticated product of an American education, destined to head one of the important units, not only of the university but of Africa. His specialty was linguistics, and he was concerned about the translation of native language into all of the sophistication of the modern world.

The mechanics of the panel meetings were set with precise detail and the determination that whatever transpired would be recorded and dealt with as objectively as possible. There were to be seven meetings of the panel. Each meeting was to be recorded and a transcript made available at the succeeding meeting. In addition, the chairman would select the highlights or possible recommendations emanating from the proceedings for discussion and inclusion in the final body of tentative recommendations.

Five consultants would be invited to present papers to the panel on various aspects of the needs of higher education in Zambia with reference to the role of the School of Education. Before the last meeting, a consultant from outside of Zambia would be brought in to examine, discuss, and present his own findings to the vice-chancellor in light of panel recommendations.

I had suspected that the expatriate representatives of the School of Education would consider the panel a necessary formality and that it would endorse what they felt was an adequate process. If this assumption was correct, they would present rather perfunctory, basic information about the school with little in the way of any new ideas for improved functioning. They would assume that the present structure was adequate. I suspected also that they would view the Zambians on the panel as necessary embellishments to the process of validating the status quo and not as involved participants in determining the structure and function of an institution that was theirs.

By the fourth meeting of the panel, a change was taking place among the panelists. Simple but searching questions addressed to the manner in which the school was being responsive to current and future needs began to be complex, direct inquiries with veiled references to possible incompetence. The Zambian representatives had begun to feel restive under the assumptions of the School of Education's implications of concordance and satisfaction with the status quo. The list was agreed upon; tentative recommendations, endorsed by the whole panel, had grown. At the end of the sixth meeting it was suggested that the next meeting should be given over to a review of the tentative recommendations so that we could delete those that were not considered fundamental to our task and add others that we felt would be more appropriate. The panel agreed.

The seventh meeting was a dilly. My secretary, Marcellina, had worked like mad to get the recommendations together and out to the panelists before the meeting. I heard the echoes of the muffled roar of outrage from the School of Education representatives two days before the meeting was to take place. They had called almost all of the panelists in an effort to get them to endorse a statement that would have declared the panel and its recommendations null and void. It didn't work. When the information was conveyed to me, I just stated that it was too bad that people entrusted with such an important task had so little awareness of what had been going on in the panel meetings.

At the meeting, the School of Education representatives asked for time to present their opposition to the panel's recommendations. I consented even though some of the panel members felt that the representatives had had ample opportunity to register any objections in prior meetings. I insisted that they be heard because it was in the interest of the panel and the future of the school to have everything laid out on the table. Privately, I felt that they needed one more opportunity to lower the boom on themselves.

They did. Their statements were fatuous and inane. It almost seemed as though they had not been privy to and party to all that had taken place. The members of the panel were indignant at the assumption that they had been considered part of a charade that was supposed to endorse the school, not seriously consider the charge put to them by the vice-chancellor, the terms of reference with which they had been presented and the accumulated number of hours they had spent in deliberation of the issue. The nuances of agreement and support that the representatives of the school had counted on to favor their position faded, and a new merger of interests had taken place. I felt a little sorry for them, but the job had to be done.

The recommendations were presented to the vice-chancellor. His feeling was that some of them could have been stronger and sharper in intent. He asked me to do that job. I asked if the pro-vice-chancellor could work with me. He had been a member of the panel but in addition was a highly respected member of the faculty and known for his devotion and loyalty to the best interests of the university. He was also an expatriate of European background.

The pro-vice-chancellor and I worked on the recommendations and the alternatives that were presented to the university. The vice-chancellor convened the Committee of Deans to review all of the information. With additions and rephrasing that put the issue of restructuring in the strongest possible terms, the committee's recommendations were brought to the floor of the Senate in a special meeting. After due deliberation, the Senate endorsed the recommendations and the first phase, the most important aspect being the restructuring of the School of Education.

CHAPTER 11

BEING BLACK IS AN EXPERIENCE!

The mining of copper is the principal industry and the backbone of the Zambian economy. It was unusual, I thought, not to have a school that would be concerned with the training of Zambians for this important part of the economic sector. Preliminary investigation and discussion with people in the know revealed that there were large numbers of Zambians employed as semi-skilled or unskilled labor in the mines, but few, if any, in supervisory or administrative positions. Almost all of these were filled by expatriates from overseas or the southern part of Africa.

It was interesting to me, therefore, when I found out that the push was on to create a School of Mines in the country. There was common agreement on the need for such a school, but not on where it should be located. This was to form the crux of an interesting confrontation between representatives of the copper mining interests, aligned with the Ministry of Mines, and the university, aligned with the Ministry of Education.

As planning officer, I was asked by the vice-chancellor to be part of the university group that was participating in a general meeting to discuss the creation of a School of Mines. The first meeting of this rather large committee was concerned with the general principle handed down by the Ministry of Mines as to the needs and values that would accrue to Zambia from having its own people trained to run the industry.

A young Zambian minor official chaired this meeting, but it soon became evident that the real power was being reflected by the Yugoslavian mining expert who was a consultant to the Ministry of Mines. He would interrupt, interpret, or define any statement or allegation presented. It was through him that the committee was given the blueprint that had been created which was to set up the school and the preferred location as seen by the expert consultants. He implied that we had been assembled for the purpose of approving this blueprint with a minimum of discussion and time since it was necessary to expedite things for the good of the country.

The vice-chancellor, as spokesman for the university, took exception to this view and held that no agreement could be reached that would automatically place the proposed school outside the university. The expert indicated that they were not trying to pressure any group into agreement but that the logic of the situation, as he saw it, precluded very much in the way of discussion of location and sponsorship of the school. The vice-chancellor stood his ground, and the ultimate decision of the committee was to create a subcommittee that would work out the details and report back to the full committee for its approval. This set the stage for an interesting and valuable involvement in the negotiations of national priorities.

When the subcommittee met the first time, I was surprised to note that I was the only black. There were no Zambians; it was a totally expatriate group. I mentioned this to the vice-chancellor. He looked at me and stated that I was the representative of the university. Did that mean that I, black but non-Zambian, could be counted on to protect Zambian university interests? Yes, that is what it meant.

Now, to me, that was a surprising development. The only

Zambian present at all meetings of the subcommittee was a male secretary to the group. How come? Well, he was not great shakes as a secretary, but he was a great "eye and ear" man. He could be relied upon to look, listen, and report, where it counted, all that transpired in each meeting.

One of the first things I do in any meeting is try to determine who is on whose side and why. Nobody comes to a meeting entirely neutral. The chairman, who represented the Ministry of Mines, made the task very simple. He opened the meeting like a person who knows where all the aces are in a card game. The ones who followed his lead represented the mining company interests. The "no trump" group represented the Ministry of Education and the university.

The "pitch" was deceptively simple. There were two understandings. First, Zambia needed a School of Mines that would endeavor to train the high level of manpower needed for the eventual takeover of the mines. Agreed. The mines were located in the northern part of Zambia on the Copperbelt. Agreed. The new School of Mines should be located on the Copperbelt. Split.

Why? The chairman was prepared for this question and proceeded to deal with it from the position of a person who has covered all the bases. In spite of the encouragement given to the university in the form of an endowment by the mining companies, it had produced only a handful of people for mining positions in its seven years of existence. Therefore, it was assumed that the university did not have the capability of producing, in quantity, the number of people that would expedite the Zambianization of the mines. The logical thing to do was to establish a School of Mines on the Copperbelt that could properly look after the interests of the country in the area of producing the people who would effect the Zambianization of the mines.

Aha! Is there another point? Of course. Certain countries are interested in helping the nation create a school that would produce people for the mining sector. They had been presented with the evidence of the university's failure and had concurred in the opinion that the school should be placed on the Copperbelt. They were ready to give aid in the form of money and personnel in order to see this was accomplished. "Is that the whole play?" That's the whole play.

I sat there listening to the utterances from those who were on the side of the chairman, trying to remember where I had run into this argument before. What was so familiar about it? By damn, it was a variation of the old "boot strap" theory. Gather some figures or statistics about the shortcomings of a group. Put them together with a rationale that is based on an existing situation where the shortcomings are illustrated. Then arrive at a conclusion that states that the shortcomings are endemic to the group. Top it off by saying other groups have had these same shortcomings and have surmounted them. What's different about this group?

The technique had been used effectively for more than a hundred years in the United States to deprive black Americans of their rights and privileges. Here it was in Zambia. More interesting than that was the source from which it flowed. The chairman was a native of an East European socialistic state. He sounded like a Bilbo from Mississippi.*

The mining representatives chimed in with their own figures and statistics purporting to support the allegations against the university and in support of the placement of the School of Mines on the Copperbelt. Their arguments were simple and direct. The sophistication of the mining industry demanded people of high

---

*Theodore G. Bilbo, a staunch segregationist and strong opponent of civil rights for African-Americans, including the right to vote, was elected as a democrat to the United States Senate in 1934 and served until his death in 1947.

education and experience. Most of these people were expatriates. Mining people should stay close to the source of their work.

Education for the mines should also be located close to the source of the industry so that it could have the benefit of the expertise of expatriates who could help with instructional chores. It had been difficult to keep educated Zambians on the job. This was due to the fact that, in most cases, they came from areas of the country foreign to the mining industry. If the school were placed on the Copperbelt, there would be a better chance of recruiting students to the school from the area. There would be a better chance for retention of the people who were trained.

Let me state at this point that my knowledge about mining education was just about zero. Living and growing up in an urban society is not conducive to taking a deep interest in the subject. These people were experts, knowledgeable about what it took to operate a mining industry. That was their turf. I was an educationist. That was my turf. The thing to do was to get them to deal on my turf.

The common denominator was education. Use the judo technique. Give enough ground to create the feeling of momentum for your adversary on his own terms; then throw him with his own momentum and your leverage. How could I create the momentum? Oh yes! I could get them to ride out the fact that I was a black, non-Zambian and get them to deal with the fact that I was American. Use the old schizoid mask. Faceless and colorless on top; black and aware beneath.

The university position was clear. This was the highest institution of the country charged with the task of creating and producing the high level of manpower for all organizations and industries in Zambia. Any educational effort aimed at producing high-level manpower had to be connected with and flow from the highest institution in the nation. The creation and development of a School of Mines had to be located within the precincts of the university, known and understood as a Zambian institution. Setting it outside of this framework would connote the fact that a Zambian-led organization could not meet the challenge of producing high-level personnel capable of handling an internationally known and recognized business like the mining industry.

Along with the representative from the Ministry of Education, we pressed for more information as to the kind of curriculum the new school would have, where the staff would come from, what they would be paid, the cost of the new school if it were started from scratch, and a number of administrative details that the chairman had not counted on having to provide. In the interest of fair play and examining all of the related issues, he had no choice but to comply with our request. He stressed the importance of settling the issue as soon as possible in order that plans could get underway. I maintained that, if the urgency of this situation had not been dealt with before now, a few more weeks could hardly make a substantive difference.

Before the next meeting, I had been able to marshal a set of facts and information that afforded me greater insight into the problem. A visiting head of state had promised assistance with projects deemed essential to development in Zambia. One of these was in the area of mining. The Ministry of Mines had developed a surplus amount of money that it wanted to use in a productive manner to further Zambianization of the mining sector.

The mining interests were aware of the fact that Zambianization was a sensitive issue, but they were also interested in production, and, to them, that meant finding a way to ensure that an appropriate number of expatriates were maintained as heads of important divisions in the mining industry. The Zambians who had qualified for positions in the mines, via their training at the university, were frustrated because the rate of advancement was slow, too slow. The reason given was that only experienced personnel could be trusted with mining operations and development. It took twenty years to get important administrative or supervisory posts. This in spite of the fact that Zambians saw young recruits with no more experience than they had given responsible positions because they were expatriates. It all began to have the ring of an old, old story.

There was one significant difference. Zambia was a sovereign nation, and its nationals were privy to the benefits derived from such status by right of inheritance and statehood. You might find ways to get around that, but you couldn't forget it or ride over it. Under the philosophy of humanism, the power resided in the people and was the people. As a black coming from a situation that was opposite, I could understand and appreciate what this meant. This was where I could make being black count in the affairs of Zambia.

When the meeting resumed, we became engaged in an exhilarating battle of wits and strategy. A proposed curriculum was presented by the chairman and one of his colleagues. I objected to it because, even to my untrained eye, it represented more nearly the training for diploma-level technicians than it did the education of degree-level personnel who could be expected to take over responsible positions. My colleagues from the Ministry of Education and the other professionally qualified representatives from the university supported this position.

The chairman explained that the curriculum was one that was used in his country. I wondered if that was a good enough reason for it to be adopted by Zambia. It was argued that the new school would train people in the specific areas of need as seen by the mining interests. I countered with the fact that the university was concerned about the breadth of the individual's educational pursuits since he would be expected to have greater mobility than a person in a more-developed country. It was stated that the rate of progress by an individual, after training, was dictated by the length of time it took to acquire the "real" knowledge that made him useful to the mines. It was suggested that, with the new and modern methods of teaching and learning, the time might be appreciably reduced.

When the costs for the new building were estimated, we maintained that the money available would not get the school off the ground because it did not include all of the adjunctive and ancillary services that an institution of higher education needed and should have in order to ensure adequate programs and development. However, with the same amount of money, the university, which was an ongoing entity with many of these services already built in, could be expected to develop a school that would more immediately fit the needs and purposes of the mines and the nation. It was estimated that the first graduates of a new school would not be turned out until late in the 1970s. I maintained that the university could produce the same number within a period of three years from 1972.

Step by step, the concept of a new school that would basically turn out technicians was moved to the concept of a university that would incorporate, as one of its schools, the study and preparation for the mining sector. The preponderance of opinion began to hold on to this version of what our task really was, and the chairman had no place to go. As soon as subcommittees, including representatives of the university and the mining sector, were formed to work out the subject components for the various divisions of mining education, I relaxed. I knew that within the near future the University of Zambia would have a School of Mines.

This incident brought home to me again the difference and similarity of being a black administrator in the United States and in Africa. In the U.S., I had to pay more attention to and use, in a very direct way, the fact that I was black. The experience of "being black" was of secondary importance to most of the people that I worked with who were non-black. That experience, however, formed a large part of my non-formal educational and life background. It was from that non-formal education that I had learned to observe, to sense, to deal with, and to outmaneuver those who had the power or authority to deprive, oppress, or exploit. If you put the first letters of those last three words together, you come up with the kind of person one can become in the States: a "DOE," a gentle, passive, conforming nonentity who can be moved at will by a stronger force or by circumstances over which he feels he has no control.

In Africa as a black administrator I was free to use and further develop the positive side of the black experience. I was not dealing with the same kind of person, but I was dealing with the same kind of thought process and attitude. Some, not all, would directly or indirectly foist upon the new nations of Africa and their institutions, the DOE effect. The connecting link between the black American and the black African is the nature and content of the "being black" experience. It is not the same for all Africans as it is not the same for all black Americans. Not to understand this is to espouse a theory that has now lost credibility in the U.S.: that the States is a "melting pot" that makes everyone the same once he becomes an American. The color "black" is not in the "melting pot" for sameness or difference.

CHAPTER 12

THE IN-BETWEENERS

Being in an almost totally black society can be as deceptive as being in an almost totally white society. Each has its myths, fantasies, customs, and traditions which, at first glance, seem genuine and necessary to the preservation and continuance of a system. Ten years of nationhood can be as binding as two hundred or five hundred years of nationhood. Between the concepts of "Black is Beautiful" and "Black is Functionally Real," there is a wide area that needs understanding and development. "Power to the People" is a slogan that rolls off the tongue very nicely. "People with Power" can stick in the craw. It is probably the difference with which a majority population, with a little persuasion, can adapt to the simplest part of the value structure with little cost to themselves against a "gut" experience in realizing that another kind of living experience has insights and substantive productivity, which one does not share in as a donor but as a recipient. It also may be whether you're just exchanging colors with the same intent in terms of carrying on as usual, or changing principles and values as to how things should be conducted. In other words, does an endemic and systemic change occur or is it just a cosmetic change?

A couple of examples may make this point clearer. At independence in 1964, Zambia was composed of vestiges of a tribal system that had ceased to operate on behalf of national unity. The colonial system had overlaid the skeleton of its operations on a land which it never expected to produce much of indigenous worth. Customs and traditions, even undesirable ones, have a habit of hanging around until something comes along to replace them. This can be a long and arduous task. Notable strides have been made in the fields of politics, social welfare, and education. But education, the first of the principles to be espoused as of value and worth to a country, is almost the last to develop the endemic changes that must accompany other forms of progress.

Thus, although there are more schools than ever before to cater to the principles of education for the masses, by and large Zambians are doing the same things in the process of education that were done by their colonial predecessors. The reason is not hard to ascertain. For every Zambian that is sent away for advanced training and techniques in learning and teaching, there are two hundred expatriates who are doing the same things they were taught to do and passing them on to hundreds of young Zambian minds. The question is not whether this is good or bad. The question deals with the fact that the training is geared to a concept which is no longer viable in a growing, developing society like Zambia.

For example, in an experiment that was carried out at the university in first-year math classes, it was found that most of the students were expert in the use and memorization of logarithms. What they had been trained to do in secondary school to ensure success in college math was out of phase with the instructors in college math who were looking for another kind of analytical skill with which to solve modern problems. If a crash course had not been instituted, most of these "capable" students would have failed, not because of lack of ability or intelligence, but because of inappropriate background and training in new math skills.

Another example will serve to point to the same problem. In the United States during the sixties, predominantly white institutions took on blacks in administrative positions to deal with the immediate concerns of black students. This was mostly a superficial gesture to equality of opportunity and black opinion. It was a cosmetic change, not a systemic change.

I can remember when the financial downturn began to be evident in many of these universities that concern was registered about the policy of bringing in qualified but poor black and other minority applicants who could not be counted upon to leave gifts of a substantial nature to private institutions or to contribute to fundraising projects of the university. At Princeton I suggested that they hire a black professional who knew the money-giving ways of black people and could direct them into university coffers. Obviously they did not understand or had no appreciation of the "dime and quarter" technique that had supported black institutions like churches and undertaking parlors for over a hundred years.

The reaction received from some of the people who took the suggestion seriously was that the people who had been recommended for this purpose wanted too much money for their efforts. I interpreted this to mean that, if it cost that much to get black parents to contribute to the institution, the only logical thing to do was to find some decent way to cut back on the really indigent students that could be taken in. After all, the argument went, the main objective was to get in qualified middle-class black and other minority students. Surely, they would be deserving of the opportunity offered and, besides, would have a better appreciation of financial obligations and objectives of the institution. In other words, a more cost-efficient process would still achieve the purpose of increasing the black and other minority student body without involving the university in a major endemic change in the way it procured money.

In order for the educational administrator to determine whether he is engaged in endemic and systemic change or in cosmetic change in an institution, he has to have what I term a concept of the theory of "open spaces." There are two kinds of open spaces. The first is occasioned by the normal growth of the institution. Not everything gets taken care of at the same time. Years can go by without anything of consequence emerging to fill the space. When it is finally worked at, whatever it is becomes basic to the ongoing purpose of the institution or organization. The second kind of open space is created inadvertently or by design. It takes care of the eager beavers, absorbs the energies of a person whom you want but who doesn't have anything specific to do at the moment, or gets rid of the person you don't want with a minimum of fuss and bother. This second kind of open space is like a bottomless pit. It can absorb just about anything without affecting the operation of the institution or organization.

A famous example of this latter kind of open space used to be to assign an ambitious group or individual the task of decreasing de facto segregation in the New York City school system, while at the same time maintaining racial balance. In Zambia they use a phrase which aptly describes to me some of the unfillable spaces, "In principle." That's like a red flag that says try it if you want to, but don't blame us if it doesn't work out. Presumably a young university in Africa needs everything it can get in order to develop its full potential for service to the country. "In principle" this is true. In fact, it isn't.

There are needs, and there are priorities. Not all needs, even basic ones, assume the nature or urgency of priorities. This is a basic fact of development, whether in Africa or the United States. Most new black administrators in the white institutions of America assumed that they were dealing with the basic need of these institutions to become more democratic in their perspective and orientation to black and other minority people. In fact they were dealing with a high-priority item to which immediate attention and energy was directed. As soon as the priority seemed to be under control or subside, it descended the scale of priorities and took its normal place in the list of needs that an institution should ascribe to or try to work toward achieving. There was a vast difference between the two conditions.

It is my belief, however, that in spite of the apparent naiveté and expectation of the black administrator that he was dealing with basic needs for democratization of the institution of higher education in the United States, his will be the ultimate vindication as to aim and purpose. The sophisticated computer systems, like PPBS and others, that have tried to determine the cost efficiency of teacher time versus student productivity, have done little to advance humanization of higher education. In spite of gigantic advances in understanding outer space and its effect on the planet Earth, there has been minimal, almost imperceptible, advancement in the nature of human cooperation and value in the building of a new society. Although the strains and tensions of the sixties have abated, the mandate for the black administrator is the same: he is and should be the cutting edge of change in the humanization of higher education. If the black administrator in the United States opts for the sinecures of status and tenure, he is, in effect, selling out the human values and principles that are important to all areas of society and the raison d'etre for educational effort.

The African educational administrator is in a unique position. He has already adopted and been co-opted by the "best" that other "civilized" educational systems can give him. I would not say that he has been disillusioned by the failure that he has experienced in trying to make these systems operate on his own behalf. I would say that he has been quicker to learn that the goals and aspirations that have been set for individual nations and for the growth of the African continent as a whole cannot be tied to or influenced by the failure of others whose ideas and concepts have not freed the human condition to reach some part of its full potential. The question may be stated as follows: Can a people, exposed to years of deprivation, oppression, and exploitation, fashion from that life survival experience, methods, and techniques that overcome difference and adversity in the creation of a common future of service?

Chapter 13

A Point in Time

In retrospect, I think that it is interesting to point out one of the important reasons that conditioned the entry of blacks into educational administration in predominantly white universities and colleges in the U.S. With certain exceptions where the financial interests of the institutions were served, educational administration was the stepchild of academia. I have heard it said on more than one occasion that "any intelligent person" could become an administrator. The incumbents were, in the main, alumni from the institution or sister institution in the same league or conference.

The assumption was that the system was already clearly defined. Aside from some minor amendments or deviation, things were supposed to run like they always had–smoothly. Even those institutions that could boast about how many blacks they had graduated usually did not invite them to become a part of their administration.

On the one hand, it is fair to state that those blacks who attended these institutions had other objectives in mind. It is equally fair to state that the administration saw no reason for them to be included in their operations. It just never crossed their minds.

The Supreme Court decision of 1954, outlawing segregation in the nation's public schools as a de jure or de facto policy of American life, had a telling effect on this situation. It was not, however, until federal legislation came into being that made it mandatory for these institutions to take in black students that the change began to occur.* The normal, intelligent white administrator did not have a clue as to the kinds of problems he would be called on to handle. It soon became apparent that the conduct of business in the same old way with a sprinkling of black students was not the answer to the multiplicity of problems that began to emerge.

Probably the most disturbing factor for most of these institutions was that, in spite of their best efforts, they could not retain more than fifty percent of the black students they recruited for their institutions under their systems and with the people that they had already given this task to. Before the black administrator was finally allowed on the scene, a number of attempts had been made to tap into black organizations like the Urban League, NAACP, CORE, and other well-known black groups or individuals to find out what they could do with their present complement of people. Undoubtedly, some valuable ideas and clues were given to them which they either could not translate into effective action or, more likely, didn't know how to interpret in the mode and culture of the new group they were taking in.

Since I was the first to get into this area of operation (the man at Yale was announced about two weeks later), I can speak with some authority about this situation. You either took the position

---

*The court orders and legislation in the 1950s and 1960s applied to public institutions only, initially to elementary and secondary schools, then to collegiate education. In the South in this same period, private colleges and universities began or continued their path to integration in parallel fashion. In the North, public and private colleges and universities were opened wider; many initiated admission and recruitment of minority students.

and tried to be as neutrally black as possible, following out the designs that had been operative for a number of years, or you tried to find out what the system was like, whether it was based on needs that you could ascertain would be of importance to black students in a real fashion, and proceeded to try to change the rules and the operations. In the first instance you might run the risk of being called an "Oreo," black top and bottom, but white in between. In the second instance you could be termed a "trouble maker," black all the way and therefore somehow devoid of the understanding that the system had to operate in a certain fashion. You were there to make sure that black students understood that or else you were "out of step" with the traditions and customs of the institution.

The educational administration of most predominantly white institutions was an in-house operation. A kind of club. Everyone knew the rules and tried to abide by them. Those who didn't weren't there very long. As a black administrator educated in white institutions, I was still outside of the Ivy League syndrome and therefore could lay claim with great validity to not knowing nor being part of their "special system." This turned out to be an important advantage at the time. It took time, of course, for it to be understood and recognized for the assets that it brought to an institution.

It also took a lot of soul searching by the people who were called on to fill the positions. Did you play the game of being the "same" as all of your colleagues? Then you would come off like one man I met who told me that he experienced no more difficulty as the representative for an important Eastern institution than his white counterpart. He represented the institution and others paid allegiance to that. Did you play the ultra-radical game? Then you came off doing and advocating things that not even the radical black student could concur with and found yourself outside of everything.

To me, black students were like other students at times. If they were unreal, then you had to deal with the fact that they were unreal. If they were on target and there was nothing built into the institution to take care of that need and presence, then you had to work like hell to make sure that something was created that dealt with them as individuals, part of a group whose needs and concerns were not met, and build that into the fabric of the institution.

Three years is a long time to be away from any changing situation, but I had the opportunity to return periodically and survey what had been happening, and my correspondents and visitors kept me fairly abreast of what has been going on. There are a lot more black educational administrators in white institutions than there were when I left in 1971. But this is no advantage if they have not adhered to their original raison d'etre. Theirs was a new perspective: the cutting edge between sameness and real difference as it affected the education and development of black and other minority students in these colleges and universities.

There can and should be the understanding in the legislative halls of municipal, state, and federal bodies that they are the cutting edge and the interpreters of what insufficient money and/or legislation means to black, other minority, and white students without the means to succeed in the old systems under which many of our legislators labored in order to achieve the thresholds of individual and corporate success. There is still no successful lobby of black and other minority educators, to my knowledge, that speaks for a totally equal set of regulations affecting the future development of this group of people in the United States.

As blacks we look to Pan Africanism and the newly developing nations of Africa to get us off the hook. That is not going to do it. As with other kinds of minorities, we are looking to the various systems of Latin America or wherever to get us off the hook and give us an example to go by. As I've seen it out here in one part of the world, they are looking to us to develop our own way and our own systems of bringing about our own deliverance and salvation. The glories of yesterday are as useful as the means we have of preserving yesterdays. The urgency is for a today that leads to a tomorrow.

If there is a reason for black American educationists in administration or other disciplines to be in Africa, it is not to carry out the well-known and well-worn systems that we already know do not operate where we are. This has already been done by our white American counterparts. The African institution of higher learning is an emerging institution that has already embarked on ways of educating people to meet its needs and demands for nationhood. "Self sufficiency" has an added meaning. It has no connotation of isolation. It is a process by which a people understands that, if they are not in command of the resources they have, or cannot control how these resources are delivered to serve their own needs, there is no place for them as nations in the society of a world, no matter what the world eventually becomes.

A case in point was the approach taken to a problem I had observed in the UNZA academic sphere soon after I arrived on the campus: the very high rate of attrition that occurred in the first two years of the natural sciences program. About fifty percent of the students who began in this area never got beyond the second year. When I inquired into the reason, I was told that they just couldn't measure up to the demands required of college students in the sciences. This sounded suspicious to me and like some of the tales that had been spread in higher education circles in the U.S. The university gets the upper one percent of the brightest students in Zambia. How come they could not handle the work required in science?

One of the facts that came to me was the nature of the personnel in the departments. There were no Zambian instructors or professors. There were British, Indians, Poles, Americans, and a few other strains from Australia or New Zealand or other parts of Africa. All expatriates. Most of them were first-rate in the knowledge of their subjects. Most of them had also come from the British or European methods of teaching and learning. This consisted almost entirely of lecturing, some tutorial sessions, and examinations given at the end of the year.

The need for scientists was among the high priorities of the nation, and the university was looked to for the production and provision of these people to eventually take over the important scientific and engineering positions. To lose half of the best that Zambia could provide was to slow down the process of localization to a minimal rate. One of the things I had to determine was whether this was deliberate sabotaging of an important need or because no better way had been found to increase the number of students who could be successful. After sitting in on several of the sessions called by the dean of the school, I ascertained that they had no better methods to use than the ones by which they had been trained and were used to themselves. It was not so much a question of not being willing to change as it was not knowing what nor how to change.

After several meetings I suggested that there were experimental programs taking place in the U.S. with which I was familiar that were aimed at the resolution of the same problems. Since I was about to go on annual leave, I would be willing to explore the nature of some of these programs and report back to the committee the ones that I felt might be most useful. In lieu of any other concrete suggestion, the dean and his special committee agreed. The proviso was that I had to obtain the consent of the vice-chancellor. I knew of the vice-chancellor's interest and concern about the problem, and when I explained to him what I had in mind, he gave me a free hand to pursue the matter.

It so happened that in January of 1972, I had been back to the

States to attend a Board of Trustees meeting of the Church Society for College Work. One of the guest speakers had been Dr. William Birenbaum, the president of Staten Island Community College. I knew his name mostly because of the publicity that had accompanied his former position as provost of Long Island University. It had been the subject of headlines for weeks.

Bill discussed some of his past educational experiences from his book, *Something for Everybody Is Not Enough.* He is a dynamic and forceful speaker. One section of his speech dealt with educational innovation and some things he had been part of in creating a community college in the Bedford Stuyvesant area of Brooklyn. This had been the locale in which I had grown up, so I was naturally interested in what had or had not been achieved.

After the speech and during the cocktail hour, I had an opportunity to ask him some questions. He was frank enough to say that some of the things he had anticipated had not come off in Bed-Stuy. That was a good opener for me because I had run into a lot of people who thought they knew what the area was like and had the solutions that would take care of some of its problems.

We were fortunate to be seated next to each other at dinner and Bill asked me where I was from. I told him the University of Zambia. He asked where I had been before that. I told him I had been Assistant Dean of the College at Princeton University. That grabbed him. He said, "You went from Princeton to Zambia? What the hell for and why that kind of move?" I laughed and launched into a brief explanation of the circumstances. Then I asked him if he had ever been to Africa. He said he had not and had tried to get there several times for educational reasons. I said that I was new in the position of planning officer there, but if anything came up that I thought he or his college would be interested in, I'd drop him a line. He evinced interest, but I knew that, as far as he was concerned, he thought it was just polite conversation.

On the strength of my discussion with the vice-chancellor, I wrote to Bill and told him that I would be in New York and that I had a proposal I thought he would find interesting. He wrote back that he would be glad to discuss any proposal I had and to let him know when I arrived and we would set up a date. When I hit New York, I called his office and was informed that he was out of town. I had a chance to speak to one of his executive assistants who was an old friend of mine, Lenny Kreisman.

I asked Len if he thought Birenbaum was interested in the subject I had broached. Len said he was but had a lot of questions. I told him I was staying at the Americana and could be reached there if Bill got back in town before I had to leave. I received a call within hours saying that he would return to the city in a couple of days and would call to set up a meeting. He did and asked if I minded if his wife, Helen, came along. I said that would be fine because I had my wife with me. We met at the appointed hour and went to Tavern on the Green for dinner.

I trotted out my portfolio of material on the university and the proposal I had in mind. I was interested in some members of his faculty in the areas of math, chemistry, and physics coming to Zambia for a limited period of time to work with and help institute new approaches to the learning of these subjects. I knew he had created several departments that were specializing in the problem of open-admissions students, and I felt that some of those techniques would be useful in our situation.

Both he and his wife were interested, and both of them asked the same questions: why Bill and why Staten Island Community College? I told them I had sized him up as a person who could take a calculated risk if the stakes were worth it. What I needed was a gambler like myself. I also told him none of the more prestigious institutions I knew of had the skills or techniques I thought would be useful, so I had discounted them as possibilities.

At the end of the dinner he had agreed in principle, but Bill said that he would like to see the situation firsthand before committing the college to any such program. I told him I understood and would start making the arrangements as soon as I returned if he gave me some possible dates when he would be available. He said he would furnish that information and we shook hands on it. That was July 1972.

By November of 1972, Bill and Helen Birenbaum were standing on Zambian soil. I had briefed the vice-chancellor and the dean of the School of Natural Sciences about the purpose of the visit. They were pleased. Things had been set in motion to bring them over. I had mapped out an itinerary for Bill and briefed him on the kinds of people he would be meeting. We threw a party for him the night before he would be moving into action and invited all of the major principals he would be seeing, including the vice-chancellor. That week was to be the turning point in the lives of many people and between two institutions.

Bill was as good as I knew he would be and better than any of the faculty expected him to be. He was low keyed, but forceful and insightful in his dealings with the heads of the various departments. Word began to get around that this was someone to be listened to, and many others besides those on the science faculty began to show up for his discussions and lectures. By the end of the week I knew we were almost home free.

The vice-chancellor gave a dinner party for Bill and Helen to which he invited the Zambians from the university who would eventually form the nucleus of central administration. It was a good group, and the gathering represented the stamp of acceptance I had hoped for. Bill and the vice-chancellor, although quite different in personality and behavior, hit it off just right. They agreed to exchange letters outlining conditions that would set up the program. The dean of the school and I were to be the liaison people to help put the agreement in motion. When the week was over, the name Bill Birenbaum was well known in the educational circles of Zambia, and the campus was buzzing with the challenges he had thrown out to them. It was decided that Peter Miles, Dean of the School of Natural Sciences, and I would take a trip to the U.S. to see Staten Island Community College (SICC) in operation and to talk to some of the potential faculty people we might be interested in. In the meantime at SICC, Bill had set up a Zambia University committee to work out the details on that end. Henry Harris, a young, black administrator, was in charge of that committee. Peter was fascinated by what he saw and heard at SICC and with the kinds of people he could envision working at UNZA. Henry and I dealt with the administrative details of the operation, what they would provide, and what we would provide to take care of the personnel involved. By the end of that week Peter had selected the people who were to come. We returned to Zambia full of enthusiasm.

Then I began to find out something about donor agencies. I knew that most of them liked to deal with well-known names in college and university circles. As a matter of fact almost all of the universities that have been involved in African educational development from the United States have been institutions like Harvard, Princeton, Michigan, Wisconsin, and Stanford. I was proposing to use a member institution of the City University of New York with whom very few in donor agency circles were familiar. By some I was called an educational heretic. Crazy. I was not fazed by that. I had been dubbed something of the same nature when I went to Princeton, but when I left, Princeton had twenty-five black administrators and more than three hundred black and other minority students. SICC had what I felt was necessary and, name or no name, it was SICC that we were going to use.

By the end of May all four of the SICC participants were in

Zambia. Charlotte McPherson, a specialist in study skills and student-teacher relationships, had arrived first. She was not only skilled, but an attractive black woman who had even the most resistant faculty members eating out of her hand by the time she left. She instituted the basic principles that were to guide the conduct of the program. Myra Hauben in chemistry, Leon Ablon in math, and Reuben Benumoff in physics were the other three. Each was different in age, personality, and response to a new situation, but all of them began to play out their roles with enthusiasm and vigor, the kind of vigor that is peculiar to Americans. Problems were there, but they dealt with them in a variety of ways and with, on the whole, more than a modicum of success. They were only at UNZA for two semesters, but by the third month the results of their work, in close cooperation with their UNZA colleagues, had begun to show success.

By the end of the six-month period I could tell from various reports that were beginning to come to my office, we were going to be successful in what we had started out to do. Zambian students in large numbers were showing they could deal with, understand, and overcome many of the shortcomings that would have ruled them out in past years as achieving science students. By the end of the academic year with most of the final exam results in, there had been a startling forty to forty-five percent increase in the number of students who had passed. In round estimates that meant instead of a forty percent pass rate, we were up to an eighty to eighty-five percent pass rate.

A good many visiting American blacks who came into my office decried the fact that there was no information in the libraries of the university or in the Ministries of Education or Rural Development that spoke to the achievements they had made in the U.S. My obvious retort was that when the people who have represented the educational interests of the U.S. have come from Harvard, Michigan,

Wisconsin, or some other predominantly white institution, one could not really expect them to tout Wilberforce, Fisk, Tuskegee, or Morehouse. The plain fact of the matter is that there is no presence, outside of West Africa, with the indulgence of the State Department, that portrays or presents as an example to African universities the dimension of educational effort that approximates some of the problems and dilemmas that many African universities face in trying to develop more relevant systems of education. The black systems in the U.S. are not seen as relevant per se to African universities because they are trying to cope with the demands of an entirely different culture.

It is possible, however, to project the imagination, perception, and innovativeness that have characterized the development of black institutions in the United States to a point where it could, in combination with African needs and inventiveness, bring to fruition that "common heritage" that is so often bruited about in nationalistic circles in the U.S. There are some blacks from the U.S. who have understood this and who have endeavored to develop industries and organizations in Africa, using their expertise gained in the U.S. to promote the desires and needs of the African continent. In the educational sphere aside from a few people who chose to go to Africa out of their own kinds of convictions or because of a strange quirk of circumstance, it is far from being the place that the informed Afro-American would choose as his venue for operations.

He is concerned, and rightly so, with his newly acquired status as a professional in his own right in the U.S. Even today that is tenuous. It may be that the black professional has to have the experience of some of his foreign contemporaries, that of running out of places to go, before he is able to put into "his heritage" that which he developed over a long period of time under adverse circumstances. It is hoped that this will not take too long. The professionals of Europe, Asia, and the commonwealth have come to Africa in droves in order to either substantiate what they think is going to be operative in the future, or to experiment with the kinds of systems and organizations they can take back to their own countries and educational systems of what is going to constitute the new ramifications of educational development in the future.

I can appreciate the genius of a Chairman Mao but do not regard it any more than the genius of Booker T. Washington or W.E.B. Du Bois in refashioning the fabric of black thinking with respect to the necessity of developing a black potential that would have its realization in the development of an America. The clear difference is that Chairman Mao was working within a system that he could influence and dictate. The genius of the black in America is that, without that dictate and in a system that was alien to himself and his way of thinking, he has still come up with the ideas and the processes that have wrought a great deal in the way of achievement in a multi-plural society in which he was low man on the totem pole. My hope is that the countries in Africa and groups of Africans will come to value the contribution that this experience can make to the development of African nationhood.

In my opinion, it will not take slogans but rather the patience to put into operation the lessons that have been learned in many ways about the value of excellence and how it survives. It will not rest necessarily on the accomplishments that have been made under adverse circumstances, but on the manner in which the lessons of that accomplishment can be put to the service of the nations that will need whatever expertise they can get from legitimate sources.

The legacy of the heritage of black America is not the money that it has developed to give to those of the same experience or persuasion in terms of their humanhood. It is lacking the manner in which there can be absolute translation of the will to survive, to succeed, and to be dominant through its adherence to the concept and practice of humanity and brotherhood. There are some axioms that transcend the ethnic, religious, or economic consideration. They may have come out of one man in one time, but they remain universal.

One such axiom is "together we stand, divided we fall." That is not only true of imperialistic or socialistic forms of government that control and condition the circumstances under which we live and strive. It is true, in a universal sense, for and about those we call "brothers."

As I used to say to the students at Princeton, "Don't plan anything today that you can't follow up tomorrow." Tomorrow is today, and each day is tomorrow. Today you plan, create, and know. Tomorrow is the fruition of what you did today. Today I am, I know, I believe. Tomorrow...?

AFTERWORD

The roles of institutions of higher education in vibrant democracies include the continuous process of welcoming the "stranger" by simultaneously reducing the barriers of exclusion and extending the circle of elites based largely upon merit. Welcoming the newcomer has never been easy or free from conflict. Indeed, the very markers of differentness may trigger fear, anxiety and a sense of loss. The challenge is to manage those markers of diversity in such a manner that both the university community as a whole and the individuals in particular increase their social capital and social imagination. Managing diversity in this sense is not a one-act drama. The markers of diversity may change, but the challenges of social inclusion are ongoing. Our will and capacity to sustain such an effort will be strengthened if we carefully reflect upon the past to identify both successes and failures. *Black in Two Worlds* provides a rare opportunity to reflect upon such challenges.

A cursory review of such U.S. national publications as *The Chronicle of Higher Education* or the *Journal of Blacks in Higher Education* underscores the contemporary relevance of this book. The following issues represent some of the current challenges of welcoming the stranger by eliminating barriers of exclusion:

- Social and economic status or class now appears to be a major marker of diversity among undergraduates that results in exclusion particularly at highly competitive universities.

- Achievement gaps between black and white students at the same institutions suggest that race remains a significant marker of diversity with negative consequences. Whether measured by grade-point average or receipt of awards for outstanding performance, a persistent gap remains between black and white students. In some cases the gap grows wider the longer the black student remains enrolled.

- Racial incidents on campuses as reported in the mass media suggest that effective management of differences and creating an atmosphere of tolerance are not one-act dramas. How to build a sustained capacity to promote social harmony on campus remains a challenge.

- Surveys of undergraduate social life suggest that perceptions of the quality and quantity of interracial relationships need improvement. Blacks are more likely to negatively perceive their social environment compared to whites. The challenge of managing diversity remains.

On the other side of the Atlantic the discussions at organizations like the Association of African Universities revolve around such issues as:

- What is unique about the identity of an African university? What is the appropriate role of the university in promoting democracy and social harmony? Are there or must there be "African" solutions to university administration that are distinct from colonial models, e.g., British, French or neo-colonial models, e.g., U.S.? How does one promote and sustain the creation of African solutions to African problems?

• What is the role and what are the core values that outline the expected social contribution of universities and their graduates? Knowledge in the service of what and whom? Can service learning be compatible with high academic standards?

• What can be done in university education to reduce the "brain drain" and social alienation of graduates who choose to leave rather than serve? How can the university promote new models of social harmony and national unity that will overcome historical patterns of discrimination and exclusion based upon national, gender, tribal, cultural or economic markers of diversity? How best to prepare university graduates to become servant leaders who adopt a practical philosophy that encourages people who choose to serve first and then lead as a way of expanding social justice. Servant leaders may or may not hold formal leadership positions; however, they are distinguished by their encouragement of collaboration, trust, foresight, listening and the ethical use of power.

The above update on issues of diversity and change in higher education in the U.S. and Africa underscores the relevance of this book. In his several capacities as administrator, leader, organizer and community builder, Carl Fields wrestled with the antecedents of these issues. Many of the elements of his success can be found in contemporary practices while others appear to be forgotten. This book gives us the opportunity to recover those ideas as we reflect upon the last forty years and prepare for the next forty. Finally, the dearth of material written by black administrators on their experiences contributes to our "historical amnesia" about how and why institutions of higher learning changed over this period. Dr. Fields adds an important piece to that larger puzzle of institutional change.

Whether by accident or design, Fields happened to be the right person at the right time in the right job in the right university. When the history of U.S. higher education in the second half of the 20th century is written, there will be a long chapter on Princeton University. Quite aside from its unusual track record in grooming numerous future university presidents and administrators, Princeton was at the forefront with other Ivy League institutions in the social desegregation of highly competitive universities. The courage and perseverance of Bob Goheen, Brad Craig, Ed Sullivan and others created an environment that permitted Fields to display his unusual talents as an administrator and communicator during an historic period of social change. (They were followed by Sheldon Hackney, Bill Bowen and Neil Rudenstine at Princeton.)

Fields was among the first to identify three distinct but interconnected phases of social desegregation in higher education, each with its own policies and programs. The first phase concerned affirmative action in the recruitment and selection of more minority students. The goal was to increase the numbers. The second phase focused on managing differences between racial and cultural groups on campus. The goal was to create processes for resolving the conflict created when "newcomers" interact with "old timers." The third phase addressed the challenge of managing diversity. The goal was to create systems that reinforced unity in diversity in the University community. Fields' innovative programs for Family Sponsors, the Association of Black Collegians and Minority Orientation were concrete expressions of his framework of analysis.

The genius of Fields' approach to working with black students at Princeton was his willingness and ability to organize them much as a labor union organizer approaches workers. He "mapped" the campus community particularly from the perspective of black students. He penetrated their circles, gained their trust and modeled the behavior of an effective leader. His method included building upon a vision of social justice, racial inclusion and social obligation to reach back to help those left behind. That vision resonated deeply with the undergraduates. It was that commitment to something larger than they that created discipline and collective action. It is no accident that many of those undergraduate leaders have gone on to achieve significant professional success including serving as trustees to the university. Most important, Fields knew well the trap of dependence when administrators intentionally or unintentionally create a circle of undergraduates to "assist" them in their duties but at the price of independence. Fields knew when it was time to say goodbye and to let the students take on the risks and rewards for becoming agents of change.

Whether at Princeton or at the University of Zambia, Fields' vision of social inclusion, racial harmony and human development remained the same. Knowledge in the service of whom and what were his operative questions. Effective action required the willingness to question the questions to which we were busily supplying answers. Distinguishing preferences from requirements represented another challenge. His efforts in working with administrators and faculty to make that distinction led to the awareness and acceptance of organizational or institutional culture as a determining factor for social inclusion and academic performance. He demonstrated that changes made to accommodate the "stranger" would benefit everyone. Indeed, the "discovery" that white students from small midwestern towns suffered comparable experiences of social exclusion and therefore deserved similar accommodations remains as one of Fields' major accomplishments. Increasing the will and capacity to create one's own processes in one's own space became his legacy.

That is the challenge of American and African higher education. The current and continuing crises of racial conflict on many U.S. campuses suggest that we would be well served to revisit the experiences of the first black administrator hired by an Ivy League university and reflect upon what contributed to his success.

It has been said that the wealth of one's life is determined by how well one learns to say hello to the stranger with warmth and how to say goodbye to a friend with grace. Such was the case with Carl Fields and Princeton University. At his memorial service held at the University chapel, three Presidents of Princeton spoke of the contributions of Dr. Fields. As I sat in meditation I could not help but be awestruck. The "stranger" had been welcomed with warmth and his friends were saying goodbye with grace. That event will be a critical incident for future historians of Princeton and American higher education. My life has been enriched by the opportunity to have been a participant observer.

Badi G. Foster, Ph.D., President

October 2005   Phelps Stokes Fund

CARL A. FIELDS
(1919-1998)

Both before and after the experiences Carl A. Fields describes in his memoir, he was dedicated to improving peoples' lives. Born on June 5, 1919 to Queena R. Grayson Fields and Ralph A. Fields in Columbus, Ohio, he was the oldest of their four sons. He grew up in Brooklyn, New York in a family and community that encouraged him to aim high and to serve others. His high achievements throughout his life illustrate that he fulfilled these goals.

Fields, a graduate of Boys High School in Brooklyn, attended St. John's University on an athletic scholarship and was a member of the first group of black students admitted there. After receiving his B.S. degree in English and Social Studies in 1942, and serving in the U.S. army, he earned his M.A. degree in Vocational Guidance from New York University in 1950, and subsequently his Ph.D. in Educational Philosophy from Philathea College, London, Ontario, Canada in 1967.

Before coming to Princeton, Fields was a vocational counselor in the Bureau of Child Guidance of the New York City Board of Education and a placement counselor in the New York State Employment Service, director of teacher placement at Hunter College and director of education for the New York Urban League. He served as an adviser to the New York State Department of Education and consultant to the New York State Citizens' Committee for Public Schools. He was a field supervisor in the National Defense Education Act Guidance Institute at Teachers College, Columbia University. In these positions, he worked with adults and teenagers, including high school dropouts, displaced workers and veterans. He was a consultant to the Metropolitan Urban Service Training Teams in New York City and an educational consultant to the New York City Youth Board Project Training

Center.

After returning from Zambia, Fields founded and was the principal partner of the African Technical Educational Consultant Service (ATEC). He assisted educational institutions, foundations and non-profit organizations in creating programs to promote the development and educational achievement of minority communities. He became the administrative officer of Riverside Church in New York City in 1984. In 1987, he became the associate director of the Bishop Tutu Southern African Refugee Scholarship Fund.

Throughout his life he received numerous prestigious awards and was frequently the first black person to do so. Cited here are some of the ways in which he was recognized for his outstanding leadership and service.

At St. John's University he was named to the Hall of Fame and was inducted into the Athletic Hall of Fame in 1988. He received their Distinguished Achievement Award, President's Medal of Honor, and University Service Award. He was the recipient of an Honorary Doctor of Laws Degree in 1989, and was awarded an Outstanding Alumni Award (posthumously).

At Princeton University he received the Association of Black Princeton Alumni's University Service Award in 1985, which was renamed the Dr. Carl A. Fields Memorial University Service Award in 1999. He was the recipient of the Alumni Council Award for Service to Princeton in 1996. In recognition of his life-long commitment to learning and to community, an endowment was created in his name for the development of the Community-Based Learning Initiative at Princeton, which was established in the fall of 1997. In 2002 the University's Third World Center was renamed the Carl A. Fields Center for Equality and Cultural Understanding.

ACKNOWLEDGMENTS

Acknowledgments usually are offered by the author to those who have contributed to the publishing of the book. In this case, I am standing in for Carl, who died July 20, 1998.

Carl began writing *Black in Two Worlds* while he was in Zambia and finished it after his return home. He was elated when the first part, about his experiences at Princeton University, was adapted in 1977 for publication in two issues of the Princeton Alumni Weekly. However, he always hoped that his description of the experience of a black administrator in higher education in both "worlds" would one day be published.

Thus, the first person I wish to thank is Hanna Fox. Many years ago, long before she was in a position to do more than make a few suggestions, Carl asked her to read his memoir. However, it stayed with her over the years and recently, now publisher of Red Hummingbird Press, she asked permission to publish it. How felicitous! Someone who knew Carl, had read the manuscript early on, and believed in it so much that some 25 years later she wanted others to have access to it.

I am deeply grateful to Bob Goheen for contributing the Foreword. There is no one more appropriate to comment on the subject of this book, no one else whose words could have more credibility. His awareness of the problems that beset the campus in the 1960s, his determination to change the course, his recruitment of Carl, and his unfailing support of Carl's efforts led to the successes achieved.

And I am grateful too to Badi Foster for writing the Afterword. Badi, as Carl recounts, was the first black student at Princeton to approach him and with that encounter there began a long-lasting friendship. Badi also was there at the beginning of the African adventure when the proposal to become Planning Officer at the University of Zambia was first broached. His own past and present work provides a unique vantage from which to reflect on Carl's experience.

Many thanks to Melvin McCray who is responsible for a number of the photographs used here. He is the author of several videos that record the history of the black presence at Princeton, the memorial services for Carl at The Riverside Church in New York City and at Princeton University, and a biography of Carl that even includes interviews with UNZA personnel. We deeply appreciate his abiding interest and expertise.

I want to thank Charles W. Daves not only for his sensitive editing of the manuscript, retaining wherever possible Carl's words, tone, and perspective, but also for his commitment, as soon as he read the manuscript, to being part of the publication process.

Those who contributed to documenting this memoir are John Danielson, John Mavros, Trevor Coombe, James Floyd, Earl Fields, Wayne and Carl Fields, Jr., Dominic Scianna, Dorothy Pearson, Daniel J. Linke, Tens C. Kapoma, the Permanent Representative of The Republic of Zambia to the UN, Moses S. Walubita, First Secretary (Press) of The Republic of Zambia to the UN, and Robert Serpell, Vice-Chancellor of the University of Zambia. Those who contributed to making it accessible are Pamela Hersh, the Princeton Human Services Commission, Kenneth Bruce, Jerome Davis, the Association of Black Princeton Alumni, and the Carl A. Fields Center for Equality and Cultural Understanding. Finally, I would like to take this opportunity to thank the many alumni, friends, and family, too numerous to name, for their unswerving support of Carl over the years and since his death.

Hedda L. Fields